The Land and People of Ireland

PORTRAITS OF THE NATIONS SERIES

The Land and People

of

IRELAND

By Elinor O'Brien

WITH AN INTRODUCTION BY
PADRAIC COLUM

J. B. LIPPINCOTT COMPANY, PHILADELPHIA & NEW YORK

Foreword

DIRECTNESS is the first quality I notice in the writing of The Land and People of Ireland, directness in the presentation of the land itself, of the normal occupations of the people, of the crises in their history that have influenced their outlook and ways of living. And this directness reminds me that the writer is young enough to have been brought up in an Ireland in which, far more than they were in the older Ireland, examination investigation technics are used. The country she writes about is a new state—or rather, a pair of new states—that came into existence in her own time. This, I believe, is the first book dealing with that new Ireland to come before outside readers.

The larger part of Ireland, now the Republic, fifty years ago was a country of landowners and tenants, with small cottages of tenants and big houses of landowners, and towns that had no business except the buying and selling of livestock and farm produce through markets and fairs. It had something too, of great interest: a traditional way of life that had lasted through centuries. The country had to meet a challenge, and, as it changed, had to meet other challenges. It is because Elinor O'Brien is aware of these challenges that, in telling what its leaders have done or are planning to do to meet them, she is more than descriptive—she is dramatic.

For the greater part, Ireland is an agricultural country, and is likely to remain one, for its metal deposits are slight and its coal

vii

deposits negligible. But its people do not want to live only in farms and in villages. And this is a challenge that the new Irish state took up. It had to give the country something of industrial life, and to do that without what had hitherto been regarded as a fundamental of industrial life—coal.

Her interest in the way this challenge is being met gives excitement to Elinor O'Brien's book. She shows us the rivers of Ireland being harnessed to dynamos to produce an industrial power that makes up for the lack of coal. And there are the bogs, too—those wide, flat, picturesque tracts that an Italian traveler saw as a wound in the body of Irish fertility. The bogs are now being turned into power and light with the design of giving the people the possibility of a variety of livelihood. As we read about these innovations we think that perhaps it was as well that Ireland remained so largely an agricultural country until the recent Age of Electricity. The Age of Steam made for huge, gloomy towns adjacent to coal mines and iron mines. With the use of electrical power there need not be such concentrations of population; towns can be small and scattered over an unblemished countryside. And with power developed from peat, parts of the country hitherto forsaken will have populations living in a new type of town. Out of this modernization a new type is arising among Irish people—the engineer and the technician.

There is another operation that Irish people look on hopefully, that is the reforestation of the country. Ireland's magnificent forests were long ago destroyed by colonists who were given tracts of confiscated lands; the sale of timber was the easiest way of exploiting these lands; the trees were cut down and there was no obligation to replant. So a great part of Ireland was left bare and denuded. Forests are now part of the Irish landscape.

Great challenges remain to test the spirit and adaptability of the people. One of them is political: in this small country there are two governments—the Republic and the Six Northern Counties' Government. How are they to be brought together and the country given a political unity without which it cannot register its full potentiality? The challenge has not been taken up, so the writer of *The Land and People of Ireland* has little to say about it. Then there is a challenge that affects the country as a whole and contains the other challenges. It is the movement of young people, boys and girls, away from the countryside. If it continues at the present rate, Ireland, including the Six Northern Counties, will become an underpopulated country, and, instead of moving forward, will become stagnant. Attempts are being made by voluntary associations to check this movement by making the countryside more sociable than it is at present. So far, the results of these attempts are not noticeable—the young people are still moving into towns or going abroad. Such attempts, however, have a way of cumulating into something effective, and a country that in the last fifty years produced several popular constructive movements can be expected to meet this challenge.

As far as towns, villages, habitations are concerned, the look of the country is changing, but the features that give Ireland its distinctive landscape remain. "May we not recognize in this the hand of bounteous Providence," wrote an eighteenth-century Englishman, Arthur Young, "which has given perhaps the most stony soil in Europe the moistest climate of it. . . . But the rocks here are covered with verdure; those of limestone, with only a thin covering of mould, have the softest and most beautiful turf imaginable." The grayness of the stones around and of the heavy clouds above makes the greenness more vivid. And the light that moves with the clouds seems, if less bright, to be more living than on other landscapes. Where there are remains from old times, they look more ancient than do the ruins in any other land.

Ireland's history is as distinctive as her landscape. In the seventh and eighth centuries she had attained a promising civilization. Its full development was checked by outside forces. The first of these was the southward and westward drive of the Germanic people, which broke communications between Ireland and European centers, and so prevented exchanges, which, coming from Europe, would have helped Ireland to stronger political institutions, and, coming from Ireland, would have helped to hasten intellectual development. The second of these disrupting forces belonged to the Northern drive also: it was the attack over a long period of the Scandinavians, the Norse, and the Danes. Centers of learning were harried; books were destroyed; learned men had to leave the country. Ireland stood up to these attacks better than did England, Scotland or France, and, under a king to whose lineage the writer of this book belongs, subdued the invaders. There was confusion afterwards, and reconstruction was interrupted. Before a new order could be created the conquerors of the neighboring country invaded Ireland. Reconquests by the Irish and reconquests again by the Normans and the English came again and again. And at times it seemed as if an Irish consciousness would be extinguished. In describing the "land and people of Ireland," it is necessary to relate these gloomy episodes. That Elinor O'Brien has related them with so much detachment shows that the people who, after centuries of effort, have been able to create for the greater part of the country a national state, have got rid of a sense of oppression. Psychologically as well as politically, Ireland is a new state.

Padraic Colum
New York City
May, 1953

Contents

The illustrations follow page 52

The Portraits of the Nations Series

Other volumes in preparation

The Land and People of Ireland

✤ 1 ✤

The Island

I am of Ireland
And the holy land of Ireland.
　　　　—W. B. YEATS

IRELAND, an island, lies in the North Atlantic between the Degrees 51.5 and 55.5 North, and between 5.25 and 10.33
West Longitude from Greenwich. From north to south it is approxi-
mately 300 miles and from east to west 150. Its area is 32,000 square
miles. According to one of the old geographies its climate is "mild,
genial and salubrious," which means that it is mild with a lot of rainfall, and healthful. An American visitor once humorously said that
in Ireland when you can see the mountains clearly it means that
rain is at hand and when you can't see them it is raining.

Ireland is shaped more or less like a bowl. Around the borders
of the country are ranges of mountains and hills, while the center is
low-lying and this area, of about a thousand square miles, is inter-
spersed with peat bogs. Among the many rivers the biggest is the
Shannon, which is two hundred miles long; and the most famous is
the Liffey, upon which Dublin is built.

In ancient times Ireland was known as the Wooded Island but
none of the ancient forest remains. Much of it was cut down to
prevent it being used as shelter in times of war, but some of the
timber was used for more worthy purposes. For instance, the great

3

beams of the roof of Westminster Hall, part of the British Houses of Parliament, were made from Irish oak.

Who the first inhabitants of Ireland were, it is not possible to say; we do know from the explorations of archeologists that the country was inhabited for six or seven thousand years before the time of Christ. Although in those early times the shape of the continent of Europe was quite different, and England was joined to France, Ireland was even then almost completely severed by great rivers and by mountain ranges. Most of the early settlers must have come by water—the Fomorians, the Firbolgs, the Tuatha De Danaan and the other half-legendary peoples, up to the invasions of historic times. Thomas Moore tells us:

> They came from a land beyond the sea
> And now o'er the western main
> Set sail in their good ships gallantly
> From the sunny lands of Spain.
> O! where's the Isle we've seen in dreams,
> Our western home and grave?
> Thus sang they as by the morning beams
> They swept the Atlantic wave.

Ireland is divided into four provinces:—Ulster in the north, Leinster in the east, Munster in the south and Connacht in the west. These provinces are subdivided into thirty-two counties, and the population of the whole is about four million.

There is a political division, too. By the terms of the Treaty of 1921 between Great Britain and Ireland, six of the Ulster counties which were predominantly Protestant and in support of Britain, should remain within the United Kingdom. This unnatural division has remained a bitter bone of contention and is likely to remain so until union is achieved.

It may be as well to point out that for over seven hundred years England tried to subjugate Ireland and make it a part of the United Kingdom as Wales and Scotland are. This attempt was never wholly successful in spite of savage persecution, confiscation of property, and on a few occasions what we today would call "liquidation." The worst attempts at liquidation of the native Irish were during the reign of Queen Elizabeth I and during the perfidious campaign of Oliver Cromwell. Following Cromwell's policy, hundreds of thousands of Irish were sold as slaves for the sugar plantations in the West Indies, as some of the Gaelic names in the West Indies today bear witness. All that remained in Ireland were given till a certain date to get to "hell or Connacht," and so to the barren hills and bogs of the west they had to go or be killed or enslaved. No race with the exception of the Jews suffered as much persecution as the Irish; and like the Jewish persecution, the Irish one was partly, and at some times wholly, religious. If, for instance, any Irish Catholic turned Protestant he was given all the privileges of the oppressor.

But perhaps the worst disaster of all to strike Ireland was the great Famine of the 1840's when more than two million people perished from hunger and the diseases that follow hunger. This famine continued intermittently for thirty or forty years and did more than anything else to destroy the old Gaelic civilization. It was during this period that the Gaelic language was almost completely wiped out, and with it many of the legends and stories and history of the race.

Within the past thirty years the face of Ireland has changed very much. The old whitewashed thatched cottages have almost all gone, and in their places we have cottages roofed with asbestos slates or colored tiles, and lighted by electricity.

The three main sources of electric power are coal, the rivers, and the enormous fuel supplies of the peat bogs. The Shannon was harnessed in 1928, and since then the Liffey, the Erne and the beautiful lakes of Wicklow have been made to yield their resources.

Since Ireland was denuded of its forests, peat has been a main source of fuel to its people. This peat, or turf as it is usually called, was until recent times cut by hand with a *slane*—a sort of triangular spade. This was a very slow process. Men who were skillful and speedy in the use of the slane were scarce and "a good man in a bog" was a term of hero worship. The slanesman flung the sods up and these sods were caught by women and placed on special barrows in a special way, and then wheeled away by young boys to the "spread ground" where they were laid to dry. As this work went on laughter echoed over the expanses of the pink heathery bog. It was healthy work and most of the workers went barefooted for the tannic acid in the bog was very good for their feet. But hand digging of the peat depended a good deal on the weather—in a wet season a large proportion of the fuel would be lost. Even in the best seasons it took a long time and many hands to secure the peat harvest.

With the growing scarcity and cost of imported coal, attention during the past few years has been turned to the great fuel reservoir of the Bog of Allen, and its industrial development has begun. For use as fuel in factories it is not necessary to cut the turf into slow drying sods—it can be used in the form of dust, called milled peat. But no matter how it is used, this fuel is light and bulky, so peat-burning generating stations are being placed as close as possible to the bog itself.

If you were to fly across the center of Ireland you would see the margins of brown featureless boglands being sectioned off with drainage ditches in preparation for excavating the peat. The big yellow digging machines follow later. They move slowly along the bog face, to and fro, as long as the harvesting season lasts.

Industrial peat development in any part of the world is a comparatively new science, and conditions vary from one country to another, so for Irish engineers this is pioneer work. Bit by bit, the machines and technique of the present day have been evolved and are being improved, so that now Ireland is able to assist other countries in finding the best way to make use of their peat resources. Bord na Mona, the nationally controlled organization which directs this work, has assembled at its Newbridge headquarters an interesting museum and the finest library on peat in western Europe.

Ireland has the smallest proportion of woodland of any European country, with the exception of Iceland, but nearly fifty years ago a Forestry Commission was set up to organize replanting. Now every season tens of thousands of seedling trees, mainly coniferous, like pine and spruce, are planted out among the heather and boulders of the mountain slopes, and the new forests are beginning to supply a useful quantity of timber, not only for ordinary purposes but also for papermaking.

But the mountains of the west coast still defeat the forester. They form a jagged frontier, nowhere more than 3,500 feet high, along most of the western seaboard, on which the damp Atlantic winds precipitate their moisture. These winds are mild, since the waters of the North Atlantic Drift, or Gulf Stream, still warm from the Gulf of Mexico, move past this coast, and help to provide a gentle showery climate in every season and to keep the grass always fresh and green. Most of the country has an annual rainfall of 30 to 50 inches, which falls on an average on two days out of every three, but on the western mountain ranges the fall is twice as heavy. Between the heavy rains and the strong salty winds from the ocean these slopes are stripped almost bare, and young trees die after a few years.

In river beds and on rocky slopes the early inhabitants found copper, gold and silver, but the accessible ores were soon stripped away. Very early, in Bronze Age times, tin had to be imported; later iron, coal and oil. Ireland has always been regarded as poor in mineral resources, but the present age has shown that anything may be useful, and prospecting is now being carried on with a new enthusiasm.

For a long time Ireland's only important industry outside agriculture was linen manufacture. The British government, at the end of the seventeenth century, had prohibited exports of woolen goods

from Ireland in order to prevent competition with their own manufacturers, and so during the next century flax growing began to gain
ground in Ireland, especially in Ulster, where land tenure was more
secure than in the other provinces. Small farmers wove their own
linen in their cottages, and could not be dislodged no matter how
prices might fall. Their product was of such high quality that an
Irish linen shirt was said to last a man from manhood until death.

Ireland's two largest cities, Dublin and Belfast, are of equal size—
about half a million each—but though this is so, Dublin still remains
the capital of the country as a whole. Belfast is a new town which
grew rapidly around the expanding linen mills and shipyards of a
hundred years ago. Dublin, with a thousand-year-old history, has a
heritage of manufacture on a medieval scale, and modern factories
are quickly springing up on the outskirts of the city. Not all new
industries are concentrating here—many have been firmly directed by
the government to provincial centers, to give more plentiful and
varied employment all through the country. Nearly every small
town now has its factory. Some are based on farm products, such as
sugar, canning, milk processing or industrial alcohol. Others, like
cement, wire products, aluminum ware, pottery, glass or papermaking, rely on local mineral resources or imported raw materials. Most
of these goods are for use at home—the only important exports are
food products.

In country towns these new factories are conspicuous. Often they
are newly designed of concrete and glass, with neat surrounding
gardens. But in some places existing buildings, the formidable cut
stone barracks, jails and workhouses of other times, have been
adapted to the peaceful progress of the present day. In Newbridge
the cavalry barracks is now used by the peat development board,
while through the gates of Tullamore prison, from which public
hangings were once conducted, hundreds of girls now pass to their
work in the worsted factory.

Because of Ireland's restless past there are few old domestic buildings in her towns and villages. The houses of today are two or three storied, and unadorned except that the plaster of their fronts is usually painted. Almost the only remarkable buildings are the ruined abbeys closed by Henry VIII in the middle of the sixteenth century, stone keeps of the type introduced by the Normans or, earlier still, tall church belfries known as "round towers."

Most Irish farms are small, under fifty acres in size—too small now that their owners want money to spend, not merely to subsist. How to make better use of the land is a constant problem. As a guide the government is setting up experimental "pilot" farms, and co-operative working is on the increase. Co-operative creameries have been established for generations—now the method is being applied in other ways. In County Waterford, for instance, little neglected apple orchards over a thirty-five mile radius have been drawn into a single unit. Spraying, manuring, transport, packing and marketing all are centrally directed, and the trees are becoming sleek, productive and profitable. Clubs for young farmers encourage interest in new techniques and are enthusiastically supported.

Root crops such as potatoes and sugar beet do well in the fertile soil. Wheat growing is officially encouraged, but wet summers introduce an element of risk into harvesting, and farmers prefer to play safe. Ireland's most useful crop is grass, which grows abundantly almost without attention. This makes the country ideal for the breeding of livestock, which can feed in the fields all year round. Where special care is given the very finest of stock is produced.

This is especially true of horses—Irish bloodstock can beat the world. Thirty miles from Dublin, on the small plain known as the Curragh, is the center of this important industry and the site of many famous stables, including the Irish National Stud. Here many champions have been produced. In the history of racing such a winner as Tulyar will be remembered forever.

✤ 2 ✤

The Small Farm

I RISH COUNTRY LIFE is based essentially on the parish, and in southern Ireland, which is predominantly Catholic, Sunday Mass is the most important social as well as religious event of the week. At the church the various streams of life in the parish meet for gossip as well as prayer—and gossip here, as almost everywhere, is the principal entertainment of the people.

After the parish church as a social center comes the parish hall, which is used mostly for dances. These are held at least twice a week. The dancing is mostly modern, to the music of modern dance bands, but occasionally folk dances are performed.

The parish usually has an amateur dramatic society. The amateur dramatic movement has spread widely during recent years and the Dublin and local newspapers devote a good deal of space to it. Drama festivals in which the various country drama groups compete are held every year; at these some well-known theatrical personality from Dublin or Belfast acts as judge. Now and again a budding actor or actress from a local group rises to the professional stage.

Sunday in Eire is also the day on which sports and football matches take place. For the young men the great game in most places is Gaelic football, which bears very little resemblance to American football but is more like rugby football that is played in England. It would be impossible to overstate the excitement which everyone

10

feels over football. Excitement is strongest when two rival parish teams meet. On that Sunday morning both going to and coming from Mass the only topic discussed is "the match." In the afternoon all roads lead to the football field and the only persons left to keep house are some of the old mothers.

In the southern counties particularly, a great sport is the ancient game of hurling. This is a stick game rather like field hockey but much more thrilling and fast; for speed and excitement it is exceeded only by ice hockey. Listen to the breathless young student in Joyce's *Portrait of the Artist as a Young Man:*

> I was away all that day from my own place over in Buttevant—I don't know if you know where that is—at a hurling match between the Croke's Own Boys and the Fearless Thurles, and by God, Stevie, that was the hard fight. My first cousin, Fonsy Davin, was stripped to the buff that day minding goal for the Limericks but he was up with the forwards half the time and shouting like mad. I never will forget that day.

Both football and hurling are controlled by the Gaelic Athletic Association, which was founded by Archbishop Croke of Cashel and Michael Cusack in 1890. The principal stadium is Croke Park in Dublin, which holds 80,000 and is packed to overflowing for big matches.

The children who live on the typical small farm go to school till the age of fourteen, which is the legal limit for school attendance, but most parents try to keep their children at school longer. If any of them show interest they are sent, if possible, to a secondary school. The girl goes to the convent school in the local town by bus or, if the distance is short, by bicycle. For boys the main source of secondary education is provided by lay monks, the Christian Brothers. The boarding schools run by various orders of priests—principally the Jesuits—are too expensive for the average small farmer. There are also some fine Protestant secondary schools such as Kilkenny College where the famous author of *Gulliver's Travels,* Jonathan Swift, was educated.

In the summer during the school holidays these young people help on the farm.

The chief outlet for these students' talents is in government offices. A large proportion of the Civil Service is recruited from the sons and daughters of the small farmers, for small farmers have a prejudice against sending their children to work in factories. Many of the girls who do not wish to go into the Civil Service or other offices take up nursing. There is a constant demand from England for student nurses and the pay during training is good. When the nurse has passed through her training she sometimes returns to Ireland to work, but most remain to staff the English hospitals.

Not more than two children of a family can ultimately stay on the small farm—the young man who is to inherit it, and the daughter who will get a dowry and marry some young man in a similar situation to her brother.

At least this has been the traditional pattern, but with the coming of the motor car and regular bus travel, country people are able to make friends far from their native fields.

Islands of the West

THE THREE ISLANDS of Aran—Inishmore, Inishmaan and Inisheer—lie in Galway Bay, thirty miles from the western capital. Inisheer is only three miles long. The biggest of them, Inishmore, is eleven miles long and has a population of a thousand.

The islands are mostly rock. Only one third of the area can be cultivated. Much even of this soil has been made by hand—a process movingly shown in Robert Flaherty's great film, *Man of Aran.* On their backs the men and women of the islands carry from the shore heavy basketfuls of sand and seaweed, which they spread carefully layer by layer until there is a skin deep enough to plant potatoes. Wind and weather wear away this man-made soil, and year by year it must be renewed. To protect the precious soil the land is parceled off by high stone fences into tiny fields, perhaps just big enough for one cow. There are no gates, and to let the cow out, a bit of the wall must be taken down. Such walls are only one stone in thickness and a false move may tumble a whole length of it.

There are no trees on the islands, and no fuel. Early each summer a fleet of the local sailing boats, called *hookers,* comes laden with turf from the mainland. To and fro past the little harbors swoop these craft, while the islanders ashore call out their bids until a bargain is made by each family. Then the turf is swiftly unloaded and stacked for the winter.

Between the islands and Galway plies the little steamer *Dun*

Aengus, carrying mail, passengers, livestock and supplies. Only on Inishmore is there a harbor big enough to accommodate the steamer. From the other islands flimsy rowboats go out to meet the steamer, swimming their cattle after them if there is livestock to be loaded. The boats, called *curraghs,* are made of canvas stretched over a frame of laths, and tarred to form a fragile armor against the sea. A curragh seems only like an eggshell, but in skilled hands and in open water it is almost unsinkable. A crew of Aran oarsmen can make one leap over the waves. To land, they race their craft at a sandy beach, the men jumping at the last minute into the surf. Then grasping the gunwales they pick up their boat and run with it out of the reach of the sea.

Barren and storm-tossed as are the islands, they have been inhabited for untold ages. The great prehistoric fortress of Dun Aengus is one of the most impressive relics of ancient Europe, while its many Christian monuments have caused the islands to be known as Aran of the Saints.

Nowhere else in the world can there be a community so distinctive and yet so tiny—less than two thousand souls. "The people themselves," wrote Sir Samuel Ferguson a hundred years ago, "so fine-natured, genial and intelligent, are more worthy of regard than all their monuments."

In spite of the sparseness and simplicity of their lives Ferguson found the islanders "handsome, courteous and amiable," and down to the present day the verdict is the same. The character of their life changes very little. Although they are objects of admiration and interest throughout the world the islanders are very poor. They have little cash to spend so almost all their needs are supplied by their handiwork. Footwear are slippers made of raw cowhide, called *pampooties,* improved rather than spoiled by frequent wettings in sea water. Clothing is made from homespun wool, woven or knitted. The men wear tweed trousers with gaily striped woolen girdles around their waists, elaborately knitted pullovers and loose white tweed jackets called *bawneens.* The women's costume is a full woolen skirt of bright red, with a neat shawl around the shoulders, crossed in front and knotted at the back. Here on Aran is the nearest approach to a national costume surviving in Ireland.

The spinning wheel for most of us is part of the romantic furnishing of a fairy story but here it is a reality in daily use. In fact the scene which the playwright John Millington Synge described fifty years ago might still be observed today:

> The kitchen itself, where I will spend most of my time, is full of beauty and distinction. The red dresses of the women who cluster round the fire on their stools give a glow of almost Eastern richness, and the walls have been toned by the turf smoke to a soft brown that blends with the gray earth color of the floor. Many sorts of fishing tackle, and the nets and oilskins of the men, are hung upon the walls or among the open rafters; and right overhead, under the thatch, there is a whole cow-skin, from which they make pampooties.
>
> Every article on these islands has an almost personal character, which gives this simple life, where all art is unknown, something of the artistic beauty of medieval life.

Besides possessing grace, charm and integrity, the islanders are a richly imaginative people. In their stories the mythology of the race is kept vital and vigorous—even their dogs are named after heroes of the past. Their daily speech is full of imagery and colorful phrases. Its character is derived from the Gaelic, which is the people's native tongue, and its dazzling quality so impressed Synge that he did his utmost to transpose it into English literature.

Although transatlantic planes pass overhead, machinery is almost unknown on the islands. Even wheeled vehicles are rare. Many of the roads are in any case only narrow lanes between high walls, sometimes not even wide enough for two people to walk abreast. It is told as a joke that when Aran men go to Galway they walk along the streets in single file, like a string of ducks.

Bitterly hard and often dangerous though life on the islands may be, it keeps its grip forever on the hearts of the Aran born. Many boys and girls to ease economic pressure at home emigrate to the United States, but they come back when they can. It is not uncommon for exiles who have lived thirty or forty years in Boston or some other American city to return for their last days to these rocky Atlantic isles.

✣ 4 ✣

A Holy Island

For though Ara was holy
Hy Brazil was blest.
—GERALD GRIFFIN

ISLANDS HAVE ALWAYS had a deep interest for the Irish imagination. Ara—or Aran—was holy but the mythical island of Hy Brazil, the Irish Atlantis, was the dream island more real than reality. What was it? Perhaps once an island indeed, far to the west of Ireland itself, which sank beneath the waves at a time when the whole northwest corner of Europe was subsiding thousands of years ago. At any rate it is believed that the missionary Saint Brendan in the seventh century searched for this island and in the course of his voyaging discovered America.

But while Ara was holy in the past and Hy Brazil caught the imagination, both these qualities are today attached to another island.

One hundred and fifty miles northwest of Dublin is the smaller of Ireland's two Lough Dergs, a lake which stretches among the mountains of Donegal. About half a mile from the southern shore of this lake is a small stony island an acre in area. This island is the celebrated Saint Patrick's Purgatory, a Christian shrine which has

17

been in existence over fifteen hundred years. From all parts of Christendom in the Middle Ages came men who had committed terrible crimes to do penance for their sins. Many who had not committed crimes came simply out of piety, as they still do. The pilgrimage opens each year on the first of June and closes on the fifteenth of August.

According to legend, on this island lived a demon who used to ravage the surrounding country. Saint Patrick, having been told of this monster, went to the island alone, where he defeated the demon, and so the place instead of being evil became holy.

In the Middle Ages a French prince had murdered his sister because she was in love with one of his knights. Then, pursued by his sister's lover, he fled to Ireland and Lough Derg. When he arrived at the shore of the lake there was no boat to take him across to the island, so he lay down exhausted to rest and wait. He was just about to fall asleep when the knight appeared above him and before the prince had time to rise he was slain.

There are many other similar true stories associated with Lough Derg, but nowadays such deeds of violence are unknown. Pilgrims no longer come barefooted but in organized groups by train and bus. Let's go there with them.

The train, radio-equipped for community prayers and hymn singing, takes us north through the little hills of Monaghan, through Fermanagh, to the little village of Pettigo. From Pettigo we take a bus up the bare mountain road and all eyes in that bus are strained for the first sight of The Island. The shrine is always referred to as "The Island."

Around us in the bus are men and women praying on their rosaries. The usual question asked of one and another is: "Is this your first time?" To which the usual answer is: "This is my tenth" or "My twentieth." Nobody who goes once fails to return. But it is our first time, and everyone is surprised.

And now there is a slight commotion around us. Somebody

through a gap in the hedge catches a glimpse of the dark waters of the Lough and then later the blue stone of the large church on The Island. To the Lough Derg pilgrim this moment is akin to a Moslem's first sight of Mecca. "Isn't it wonderful!" everyone cries, as he goes down on his knees and makes the Sign of the Cross.

There is not much time lost in reflection. The boatmen have a huge rowboat pulled in to the simple pier. This boat holds one hundred and fifty people and is rowed by eight strong men. Motor boats are not allowed.

As we near The Island our excited eyes are watching other excited eyes on its pier, for new pilgrims never fail to be an adventure. The pilgrim on The Island is a man in another world as we later learned, and we, the new pilgrims, are bringing news of our ordinary world. We will bring news to these people of the hay harvest, and who won the football match the previous day.

Already some of the pilgrims in the boat have their shoes off. You take off your shoes and stockings before landing.

And here we have landed on The Island and are all ready to start our religious exercises, or the Stations as they are called. We have made it our business to know all about the Stations before coming. We have been fasting from the night before and cannot have our first meal till we go through a Station.

It takes about an hour to perform a Station. The Station consists of going round the Basilica seven times while we say a decade of the Rosary each time. Then we pad around on a series of "beds" which are rings of sharp stones, praying all the time. We have scarcely time to notice the one stunted tree on The Island, or the little green knoll upon which in the summer sunlight a group of pilgrims reclines gossiping.

At last our Station is ended. We are entitled to break our fast. We are ushered into a long refectory, where we are served black tea and pieces of dry toast. This is our only meal of the day and yet everyone present is enjoying himself as if it were a great banquet.

Out into the sunlight we go again for more prayer.

We do not go to bed the first night but keep vigil in the Basilica. It is worth losing this night's sleep if only that we might watch the sun rising over the hills of Donegal.

Our second day is similar to the first. On the second night we get to bed.

On the third and last day we have to be up early to do our final Station and be ready to take the boat which leaves at noon. We are hungry and tired as we put on our shoes. We can have nothing to eat until after midnight and yet we are excited. We have been out of the world for three days. As the boat moves off the hundred and fifty pilgrims join in the pilgrims' hymn:

> O fare thee well, Lough Derg,
> I may never see thee more;
> My heart is filled with sorrow
> To leave thy sainted shore.

✤ 5 ✤

From Shellfishers to Scribes

EARLIEST MAN in Ireland probably lived about six thousand years before Christ. He has left hardly any evidence of his existence or his habits apart from some deposits of sea shells embedded in the soil or sandhills on the northern coast—the refuse from his simple meals.

As the centuries passed the cultures of various parts of Europe contributed to the progress of their western outpost, but the population of Ireland was growing into a vigorous and intelligent community which could not only seize on a new idea but could give it a form all its own. There are distinctive patterns of tools, ornaments and sculpture, for instance, which are native to Ireland, like the crescent-shaped gold collars so finely decorated with geometric designs.

The first monuments which these early inhabitants have left to us are their burial places. It must have taken the whole efforts of a primitive tribe to erect some of the tombs which mark important graves. Even the simplest dolmens—usually three elongated boulders supporting a tilted capstone—must have taken tremendous labor and skill to build so that they still stand solid after perhaps two or three thousand years.

Of all these memorials the finest is at Newgrange by the Boyne River, not far from Tara, metropolis of pagan and early Christian Ireland. Here stands a man-made mound over forty feet high—some

50,000 tons of stone. Today the mound has subsided a little and is grown over with thornbushes, but originally its entire surface was sheeted with glittering white quartz brought from distant quarries.

Leading to the heart of this mound is a twenty-yard-long narrow passage, and in a central chamber are three recesses, each containing a stone basin, designed apparently to hold the ashes of departed kings. In the course of passing centuries the tomb has been plundered, and almost everything transportable removed from this noble monument, but built into it are boulders decorated with triangular, spiral, zigzag and lozenge patterns cut into the surface of the stone.

Some time after 2000 B.C. the Bronze Age reached Ireland, and exposed the lack of a very important metal. Copper was plentiful enough, but there was no tin. However, it was available not far away, and Irish traders brought the necessary supplies from the west of England. They had a strong interest in the Cornish tin mines and perhaps even complete control of them for a time. At any rate by tradition the patron saint of the tin miners there to this day is an Irishman. His name was Ciaran and he sailed to Cornwall—legend says—on a flagstone. He gathered some disciples there, who in their slightly different Celtic dialect knew him as Piran and he established a church in a place now called Perranzabuloe, near the sea. But he happened to find tin in the sea sand, and he and his followers became more interested in streaming for tin than in their religious duties, and gradually the sands drifted over their church until it disappeared from sight. On hearing that the local bishop was about to pay a formal visit the monks made a desperate search for the church, and discovered a gable end just in time. They knelt around it and prayed hard, and when the bishop arrived Piran explained to him that they had buried their church specially to keep it extra safe.

The old church, deep in the sand, was rediscovered just over a hundred years ago.

Population movements in Ireland during the thousand years before the birth of Christ are the subject of speculation, and facts are few. The Celtic language and social organization were strong in western Europe and came to dominate Irish life, but whether through an invading European force or through the spread of ideas cannot be said with certainty. Not until the coming of Christianity was any form of writing used—law, legend and history alike had to be transmitted by word of mouth from one generation to the next. The memorizing and interpreting of the legal system was the task of specially trained experts known as *brehons,* while every chieftain had attached to his household a bard whose responsibility it was to put into metrical form which could be memorized the important events of the day.

In the course of time some of these works were written down, but the one great Irish epic known as *The Táin* or Cattle Raid of Cooley, for instance, was several hundred years old before it was put on paper, and the elaborate system of the Brehon Laws had been out of use for a long time before it was written in early manuscripts. However, we do know that these laws were very carefully worked out and regulated every aspect of life in the community. Politically they provided for more than a hundred units of territory, each ruled over by a chieftain, but by degrees some of these units became strong at the expense of others, until the country was divided into five kingdoms, or provinces. After the year 200 A.D. there was a central high king, but he had no machinery for unified government—no central armed force, no towns and no efficient transport to link up the scattered population. High kingship became the perquisite of the most powerful provincial government, which made use of the office to extort taxes from the other provinces.

Stories—half legendary, half historical—about the outstanding men and women of those times have come down to us, and the adventures of Cuchulain, of Finn and his companions, Diarmid and Grannia, Deirdre and the sons of Usna, Maeve and many others, were an inspiration to the Irish literary movement of fifty years ago.

Meantime on the continent of Europe the Roman legions were

conquering all before them, but although they ruled England from the first to the fifth century A.D. they never came to Ireland. Then as the Roman retreat from northern Europe began, the Irish took the opportunity to raid Britain's western approaches, where they held large areas and left Scotland completely Gaelicized.

As the Roman power waned the new ideas of Christianity gained ground. After the year 400 a marauding expedition of the high king Niall brought to Ireland from the west of England a fifteen-year-old boy named Patrick. He was put to work tending sheep for a farmer on the north coast, but after six years he succeeded in escaping to France. Here he studied the Christian faith and in 432 returned to the pagan island—this time as a missionary.

There were no martyrs among the first Irish Christians. Christianity filled a need both spiritual and social which had never been met by the old Druid beliefs, and to make the transition even easier many of the external features of the latter were given a Christian significance. The old festivals were given new names.

When Patrick arrived in Ireland he went directly to Tara to interview the high king, Leary, the son of Niall who had carried him off as a boy. Leary was interested and sympathetic towards Patrick's point of view, and although he did not himself become a Christian he raised no obstacles to the missionary campaign. He was in fact glad to have the opportunity of discussing affairs with this intelligent and cosmopolitan European, and of getting his advice.

When he had consolidated his position in the territory under Leary's control, Patrick traveled farther afield, meeting as many important people as he could and trying to win their support for the new faith. But a religion which preached equality also captured the imagination of the less privileged, for the strict regulations of Gaelic society meant that a section of the population lived in hereditary bondage.

The Druid priests naturally opposed the new religion with their strongest arguments and for a time held the allegiance of an important section of the population, but before long the whole country had accepted the new faith.

Besides the Druids its chief opponents were the members of the bardic order who could see in such innovations as the art of writing a threat to their own existence. But before long the bards had reason to be grateful to an enlightened Christian, Columkille, energetic founder of early monastic settlements.

By exploiting their privileged position and their literary skill they had become highly unpopular with the ruling families who maintained them. Should any patron refuse an extravagant request he was publicly satirized, and so exuberant and irresponsible did the bards become that at the end of the sixth century the reigning high king decided to abolish the whole order.

This threat caused consternation—it was almost as if in our own time the newspapers were threatened with suppression. An assembly was arranged at Dromketh, in County Derry, at which high king, princes, clerics and bards were to argue the matter out. Gaelic poetry and music were at stake—for the bardic compositions were sung to the music of the harp—not to mention the status of a large number of people. There were then something like twelve hundred bards in the two provinces of Meath and Ulster alone.

Columkille, busy in his important monastery on the Scottish island of Iona, hurried back to Ireland for this gathering, although in dedicating his life to missionary work he had intended never to set foot in his native land again. But he felt keenly on the subject of the threatened arts, and at Dromketh he spoke eloquently on behalf of the bards. His influence was decisive, and on certain reforms being promised, the order was reprieved.

For centuries after this event the Irish poets remembered Columkille with affection and gratitude, and gracefully attributed to him some of their most charming verses. His tireless activity in transcribing verses is recalled by a writer of some thousand years ago:

> My little dripping pen travels
> Across the plain of shining books,
> Without ceasing for the wealth of the great—
> Whence my hand is weary with writing.

Lines such as these were written in their native Gaelic by monks who had dedicated their lives to the transcription of the Gospels, making copy after copy of the Latin text. In those times, before printing, the devoted scribes made a point of carrying out this work as beautifully as possible, and in illuminating manuscripts the Irish monks excelled. On vellum and with colored inks they found a new outlet for the national talent for decoration, and the Book of Kells, which still survives from this period, is one of the artistic marvels of the world.

As Christianity advanced in Ireland it suffered setbacks in Britain and Europe. Waves of Germanic invaders, bringing paganism and disorder, swept across the continent in the wake of the collapsing empire of Rome. The newly converted island was isolated for more than two centuries, and the Irish church developed along distinctive lines. Politically the country was almost completely unorganized and recruits to the new faith, exhilarated by the ideas it brought them, preferred to isolate themselves in communities devoted to scholarship rather than to exercise authority on the social life of the country.

During the eighth and ninth centuries the monastic centers flourished. Their members studied, taught and reproduced the Gospels. They were able to send missionaries to paganized England, France, and even as far as Switzerland; these missionaries established monasteries and distributed religious manuscripts.

Among them were some adventurous and stimulating thinkers and pioneers of science. Feargal, the geometer, later Bishop Virgilius of Salzburg, put forward in 750 the theory that the earth was a sphere, while the astronomer, Dungal, was able to explain an eclipse of the sun to the French Emperor, Charlemagne. Diciul, who went to France in 810, wrote a book called *De mensura orbis terrarum,* which was a geography of the then known world, from Iceland to Egypt. But the most important of these scholars was John Scotus Eriugena, who joined the French court of Charles the Bald, where as teacher and philosopher he proved an explosive force.

At home, as well as the important teaching centers such as Clonmacnoise and Armagh, where the number of students ran into thousands, there were many lonely settlements in which anchorites tried to practice their conception of Christianity. On barren rocks and islets they built low stone "beehive" huts, some of which still survive, the most remarkable being the little colony on the spiky rock of Skellig Micil off the Kerry coast.

But while these hermits deliberately looked for hardship and loneliness they could not help enjoying the beauty of their surroundings, and on to the margins of the precious manuscripts on which they toiled would spill over some of their pleasure in life.

> Delightful I think it is to be in the bosom of an isle
> On the crest of a rock . . .

Others chose quiet spots inland, like the lovely Glendalough Valley, making use of the wild fruits in season to add to their modest diet.

> All a man could ask of comfort
> Round me grows,
> Here are hips and haws and strawberries,
> Nuts and sloes.

Even the most solitary hermit had company—a pet cat, wild creatures that had become friendly, and small song birds.

> My little bard, my man of song,
> Went on a foray all day long,
> Three midges were the poet's prey,
> He cannot eat them in a day.

As the scholastic and missionary activities of the Irish monks reached their height, ships began to leave the shores of another part of Europe. Pressed by a growing population and hard economic conditions at home, Danes and Norwegians were setting out to seek their fortunes abroad. These efficient seamen and determined warriors fastened on the more accessible parts of Britain and Ireland, later sweeping on to sack Paris, attack Spain, and even penetrate the Mediterranean.

In Ireland there was no organized force to withstand them, and they were able to settle at will on the coasts and waterways, first plundering and destroying, later founding the first Irish towns—Dublin, Wexford, Waterford, Limerick and many others. The monastic centers, being not only the most vulnerable communities but also the storehouses of most of the treasure and craftsmanship of the country, were the main targets for attack. The pagan Norsemen had no respect for their sanctity.

The monks who had sought lonely and difficult places in which to live now found themselves face to face with real and terrible danger, and the Irish church had its first martyrs.

Monastic life became an uneasy affair, and the scholar, working with an ear cocked for danger signals, could be glad of a storm.

> Bitter is the wind tonight,
> It tosses the ocean's white hair;
> Tonight I fear not the fierce warriors of Norway
> Coursing on the Irish sea.

✤ 6 ✤

The Norsemen

NEWLY ESTABLISHED TOWNS, at first fortresses for the invader, soon became centers for the native population as well. From their enemies the Irish learned the art of trading, while the Norsemen began to adopt Christianity and founded a number of churches, including Christchurch Cathedral in Dublin. Intermarriage became common as the raiders' status changed to that of colonists, and they began to adopt Gaelic customs. The prefix Mac or O (meaning son or descendant) began to appear before Nordic names.

The towns challenged the old pastoral life of the chiefs and their whole conception of wealth and property. Livestock had been the currency of the country—taxes were collected and gifts were made in the form of cattle and horses, a system so cumbersome that any sort of private wealth was almost out of the question. But the Norsemen in their first onslaughts had gathered in all the gold they could lay their hands on, and used it to import luxury goods from their bases abroad. Silks, jewelry and wines became the perquisites of the rich and strong, and the influence of the chiefs increased with their stocks of foreign valuables.

At the same time the Norsemen were becoming by degrees more and more closely involved in the local politics of the Gaelic chiefs.

The political pattern in the country was an uneasy one, based on a patchwork of some hundred chiefs, divided among five or six provinces, while the provincial rulers competed with one another for the high kingship of the whole country. While such decentralization had proved an obstacle to Norse conquest of the country, individual rulers did not hesitate to make use of the settlers in quarrels with their neighbors—for instance the kings of Leinster enlisted the aid of the Dubliners in their struggle against the adjoining province of Meath.

Brian Boru, high king of Ireland from 1002 until his death in 1014, might be described as the first Irish statesman. He regarded the country as a single unit, and understood the importance of a centralized government, of trade and shipping, of a unified administration of the church, and of a modernization of social customs.

Brian was a member of the ruling family of an obscure tribe in Clare. His elder brother, in the course of a distinguished career, became king of the province of Munster, but was murdered by a jealous rival with the assistance of Ivar, the Danish lord of Limerick. Brian avenged his brother, and became in his turn king of Munster. Then slowly, using both force and diplomacy, he won support throughout the country, until at last he was in a position to challenge Malachy, the reigning high king. He offered the alternative of a pitched battle or abdication within a stated period.

Malachy, fond of good living, hard riding and practical jokes, generous and good natured, was no match for the ambitious Brian. At the end of the time allowed he visited Brian's headquarters and gave up the high kingship without conditions. The arrangement was a completely amicable one, and the two remained good friends. Malachy was able to devote more time to riding unmanageable horses and broke a limb at this occupation when he was over fifty.

Brian was a strong ruler, and during his reign established comparative order and security throughout his realm. He helped to restore the monasteries, which had not only been plundered during Norse raids but had also been damaged in the course of intertribal and interprovincial quarrels. Monasteries had come to be regarded often as the private property of ruling families and their sanctity was not considered.

Brian also did what he could to improve transport by repairing roads and bridges; and to help administration he introduced the use of surnames, his own descendants becoming known as O'Briens.

In spite of his powerful position, Brian could not escape the jealousy and resentment of some of the lesser rulers, notably that of the king of Leinster, whose province had for generations been subjected to exceptionally severe taxation by the high kings at Tara. Brian had come to be known as Brian Boru, or Brian of the Tributes, because of the burden of taxation which he exacted from subordinate leaders.

Eventually Maelmorra, the king of Leinster, tried to form an alliance with the Dublin Norsemen in order to challenge Brian's supremacy by force. However, the Dubliners had by this time become so well established in the country that they had no interest in upsetting the existing regime. But, although they were reluctant to take sides in the issue, another Norse colony welcomed the news of discontent in Ireland. These were the Danish settlers in the Orkney Islands, north of Scotland. Their leader, Sigurd, had been unsuccessful in his attempts to subdue the Scottish kingdom, and he decided to take this opportunity to carve for himself a foothold on Irish soil. With the help of the Norse settlements on the coast and islands of Scotland, from the Orkneys to the Isle of Man, he mobilized a fleet for this purpose.

It was this force, allied with that of the king of Leinster, which met the army of Brian Boru at Clontarf near Dublin on Good Friday of the year 1014. It was a decisive day in Irish history, and the defeat of the invaders put an end to Norse hopes of an Irish conquest.

✤ 7 ✤

The Normans

THE FIRST small company of Normans to arrive
in Ireland in 1169, with the help of their Irish allies, had little difficulty in overcoming such resistance as was offered. Tanks used against
spear-carrying tribesmen could hardly be more effective than were
the Norman warriors with their coats of mail and accurate long-
range weapons. The crossbow, with a range of up to 100 yards, was
so deadly that the Lateran Council of 1139 had condemned its use
against Christian enemies. The longbow had an even greater range.
Battering-rams, giant catapults and other weapons had been devised
for assaults on towns. Above all, the Norman troops were widely ex-
perienced and highly disciplined.

Against this force stood Irish part-time soldiers, lightly clad, without armor, and proud of their agility with short-range weapons such
as sword or axe. The Normans sliced through this amateurish opposition, and quickly established themselves in bases on the east
coast.

Within a few months, in 1171, Henry II of England himself came
to Ireland, not only to supervise the campaign but also to make sure
that the colonists were not becoming too powerful and independent.
He even then anticipated what was in later centuries to be the
scourge of the English crown—the transformation of each successive
wave of settlers into a force with interests opposed to Britain.

Henry was welcomed by the church and readily acknowledged as sovereign even by some of the Gaelic rulers in south and east, who regarded him as a more reliable upholder of their positions than the ineffectual claimant to the high kingship at the time, Rory O'Connor. Henry accepted their submission, entertained them lavishly at Dublin—and gave away their lands to his Norman barons.

The Irish chiefs were powerless to prevent the appropriation of their estates, and the Normans quickly consolidated their hold by building castles. The first were of wood, placed on fortified mounds, but these were soon replaced by stone fortresses, many of which survive to the present day.

We have a very good idea of what the Normans thought of the Irish in the first days of their invasion. A Welsh Norman named Gerald Barry visited Ireland in 1183 and again a couple of years later, and wrote a little book about the country. In the midst of highly colored travelers' tales and prejudiced comments there are some genuine personal impressions of how the people lived.

As a race he considered the Irish to be generally handsome and athletic in build, but he found them very careless about personal appearance. Hair and beards were allowed to grow long, and clothing was usually made of the natural wool of black sheep. Men wore close fitting hoods which came down over their shoulders, a tunic and trousers.

Barry complained of the lack of refinement in the manners of the Irish, but they had one social gift over which he became enthusiastic. He had never heard anything so lovely as their music, so sweet and lively. Their principal instrument was the harp.

Religious standards he found low, and blamed the monastic tradition of the Irish church. Monks looked after themselves alone, he pointed out, but clergy were responsible for the care of many. At the same time he admired the great art which the monks had applied to their manuscripts. "Look closely at one of these designs," he wrote, and "you will notice such intricacies, so delicate and subtle, so close together and well-knitted, so involved and bound together, and so fresh still in their colourings that you will not hesitate to declare that all these things must have been the result of the work, not of men, but of angels."

He found the economic system in Ireland very backward, based as it was on the grazing of great herds of cattle, rather than on the cultivation of the soil. As a result the main item of diet was meat, which disgusted him. The only significant export was hides, while wine and other luxuries were imported. He wanted to see more attention given to apple growing, and the introduction of better varieties. Mineral resources too should be developed, and he disapproved of the contempt in which domestic crafts such as weaving were held.

But during the centuries which followed the two ways of life merged. As the Normans adopted some of the customs of the Irish, the latter learned from the settlers the arts of building castles and waging war. In spite of conflicts, however, a more or less stable community life grew up around the castles of leading families, both Gaelic and Norman. Agriculture became more varied and trades developed. Church organization was brought into line with European practice, and gradually English law replaced the Gaelic Brehon system.

✤ 8 ✤

Plantations

ENGLAND'S WEALTH and strength continued to increase. Her navy became invincible, the world was her market place, and during the reign of Henry VIII policy towards Ireland hardened.

In Ireland the old Gaelic order had crumbled and had been replaced by no central organization. Landowners held on to their property as best they could. Some followed such militant leaders as the Gaelic O'Neills or the Norman Fitzgeralds—others were prepared to swear allegiance to the English king. Allies were befriended and betrayed as the occasion demanded. Brother fought brother, marriage became a form of strategy. But no combination was strong enough to resist the mighty pressure from the neighboring island.

Henry's tactics were at first discreet. Many of the great landowners were permitted to hold their estates on condition that they exchanged their Gaelic titles for English ones. This seemingly harmless transformation was carried out in Greenwich, near London, with great ceremony. The king placed gold chains about the necks of such Gaelic leaders as Conn O'Neill, who became Earl of Tyrone, and Murrogh O'Brien, who was made Earl of Thomond. But when the new earls returned home they found their followers far from pleased that hereditary leadership had replaced the old system of election by the clan.

The other serious change which took place during Henry's reign was the attempted suppression of the Catholic faith. The king, having renounced the supremacy of the pope and proclaimed himself head of the church, put his own nominees in key positions in the hierarchy and ordered the monasteries to be closed.

Under Henry's decree the monasteries were abandoned, although the roofless ruins of very many of these beautiful buildings are still to be seen all over Ireland. Their dissolution brought a new mode of religious life—the old self-contained community belonged to the past, and now monks and priests had to go out among the people, often in disguise and in peril of their lives.

Henry was succeeded first by his son, Edward VI, and then by his daughter, Mary, who restored for a time the old faith but did not relax the tighter grip that had been gained in Ireland. In fact she was responsible in the 1550's for a new and more thorough method of colonization, which became known as "plantation." In the area represented today by the two counties of Leix and Offaly she ordered the complete clearance of the ruling families, the O'Connors and the O'Moores. She gave their estates to English settlers, renamed the territory Queen's County and King's County, and called the principal towns Maryborough, after herself, and Philipstown, in honor of her husband, Philip II of Spain.

In such planted areas the new owners were supposed to bring retainers with them from England to do the farm work, but in practice this was usually impossible, and so many of the natives who were not important enough to have been moved remained in their old situations and grew food for the new landlords.

In Elizabethan England exploration, plunder and piracy went hand in hand. Success was generously rewarded, perhaps at the expense of someone whose achievements were out of favor or simply out of date. Estates in Ireland were bestowed openhandedly. Sir Walter Raleigh, soldier and courtier, who introduced to Britain tobacco and potatoes, in addition receiving the privilege of selling licenses to wine merchants, was presented with tens of thousands of acres of Munster land. Edmund Spenser was given three thousand acres of rather poor land on the borders of Cork and Limerick—a reward not so much for his poetic genius as for his clerical services to the Deputy, Lord Grey.

Spenser was oppressed by the desolate condition of the people and longed for the sophisticated atmosphere of the court in London. He watched with sorrow the wasted peasantry coming from their hiding places in the woods as the terror subsided, "creeping upon their hands, for their legs could not bear them," feeding on shamrocks or water cress, and dying on all sides of starvation. But in his crumbling castle in County Cork he wrote part of *The Faery Queen,* and invented too, some pleasant fantasies about his natural surroundings. Eventually his home was accidentally burned, and he returned to England.

✦ 9 ✦

Kinsale and Cromwell

O'er many a river bridged with ice,
   Through many a vale with snowdrifts dumb,
Past quaking fen and precipice,
   The Princes of the North are come.
                              —AUBREY DE VERE

IN THE NORTHERN counties the powerful O'Neills held their own, half friendly, half defiantly, against Elizabeth. Shane the Proud visited her court, but as a ruler of equal status.

His successor Hugh was educated in England and grew up to serve the queen like any other aristocratic adventurer of his time. He took a hand in the suppression of the revolt of the Norman lords in the south, but of the Irish chiefs he was by far the most able, and became known as the Great O'Neill. Although for a time there was no open breach, Elizabeth's advisers did not like to see any Irishman making a name for military prowess, and he soon found his own northern territories menaced.

Hugh O'Neill's resistance was the most serious challenge to English domination in many generations. He built up his position with great caution. He was permitted to keep an armed force of only six hundred men, but by frequently disbanding this retinue and enlisting fresh batches he was able to train a considerable number of his followers. On the pretense of requiring roofing material for his

38

castle he imported lead which he had made into bullets.

In 1594 he began to harry the English forces. He appealed for help to Philip of Spain, and it was the arrival of meager Spanish aid in 1601 which brought his campaign to its climax.

The battle of Kinsale is one of the great turning points in Irish history—a glorious although a tragic one. The Spaniards were penned in this south coast town by an English army 13,000 strong, and in a heroic winter march by a seemingly impassible route O'Neill brought his men from the north to relieve the garrison.

The bold stroke failed. The northern resistance was broken. O'Neill was no longer great, and before long he and his allies relinquished their claims and sailed for the continent—a departure romantically known as the Flight of the Earls.

There was little romance left in Irish life at this time. Even the bards, who in former days had sung the glories of their feudal lords, were now parasites living off the powerful usurping families, dispensing flattery or malice as the occasion demanded. As the Gaelic leadership toppled, bardic ridicule increased to such an extent that it was encouraged by English officials, who found it a useful weapon in discrediting their enemies.

Ulster like the rest of the country was now portioned among settlers, most of whom came from Scotland. It seemed as if Ireland had been finally subdued, but meanwhile England itself was in a state of unrest.

Its Protestant middle class, growing rapidly in numbers and strength with the development of foreign trade, wanted a voice in the running of the country. They were anxious to see a democratic parliament with real power, instead of a body which could be assembled and dismissed to suit the whim of the monarch.

The autocratic governments of Europe watched this development with keen interest and apprehension. Ireland to them represented a useful tool in bringing about the defeat of England's upstart merchant class with its dangerous ideas. The exiled Irish leaders received sympathetic support in France, Spain and Rome, and in 1641 the struggle broke out afresh.

Owen Roe O'Neill arrived with reinforcements from the continent, and a political assembly was established, known as the Confederation of Kilkenny. This was Ireland's first parliament in which all sections of the community were represented, and it remained in existence for seven years. But they were years of fighting, and it could not do much more than voice the protests of the Irish leaders against the English regime. Even in this the confederation was restricted. Not all its members had the same point of view. The Gaelic representatives wanted to have their lands restored—others had uneasy memories and preferred not to discuss the subject of rightful ownership. But all were united in protesting to the English king against the persecution of Catholics, which was becoming increasingly severe.

It soon became clear that they were demanding from the king something that it was not in his power to grant. While the Confederates were hitting out at his forces in Ireland, across the water the royalists were taking heavy punishment from the parliamentarians. Discontent had turned to open revolt, a revolt which had nothing in common with the rebellion in Ireland. The parliamentarians had no sympathy whatever with the cause of the Confederates.

1649 saw the execution of Charles I, and the arrival in Ireland of Oliver Cromwell. That year, too, Owen Roe O'Neill died—poisoned, it was rumored.

> "Did they dare, did they dare to slay Owen Roe O'Neill?"
> "Yes, they slew with poison whom they feared to meet with
>   steel,"

wrote Thomas Davis.

Ireland lay defenseless before Cromwell. The citizens of many towns resisted desperately but hopelessly. No quarter was given—

civilians, women and children were slaughtered with the garrison forces. It was one of the most terrible campaigns of extermination in human history. In four years one third of the population had perished from famine, war or disease. Thousands more were shipped to the West Indies as slaves—20,000 in 1653 alone.

To "hell or Connacht" with the Irish was the order ceremonially proclaimed to the sound of drums and trumpets on the eleventh of October, 1652. It was rigorously enforced. Throughout the winter thousands of families, rich and poor, Gael, Norman and planter, were hunted across Ireland to the barren seaboard province, leaving their homes and farms to be seized as prizes by Cromwell's soldiery.

With Cromwell's death in 1658 the terror was relaxed, but down the centuries his name has not ceased to be execrated in Ireland.

✤ 10 ✤

The Battle of the Boyne

July the first of a morning clear, one thousand six
hundred and ninety,
King William did his men prepare, of thousands he
had thirty;
To fight King James and all his foes, encamped near
the Boyne Water,
He little feared, though two to one, their multitudes
to scatter.

THIS BATTLE on a summer's day in 1690, in a
setting long hallowed in Irish memory, was one of the most spec-
tacular episodes in the country's history. Close by lay the prehistoric
tombs at Newgrange, the royal burial ground at Rosnaree, and Tara,
where once stood the palaces of the kings of Ireland.

Here on the grassy banks of the River Boyne gathered the opposing armies (not so ill-matched in numbers as the ballad would suggest) of rival English kings, to settle an issue which had very little to
do with Ireland's cause.

Although the Catholic James II used religion as a rallying cry,
and the Irish cause became identified with his defeat, in fact Irish
soldiers fought also on William's side—and enjoyed the benefits of
better leadership. James was a poor soldier, and having no interest
in the fate of his Irish allies, literally ran from the field as he saw
that the day was going against him.

"Change kings and we'll fight you again!" his Irish commander
Sarsfield is said to have called to the victorious Williamites.

42

James galloped to Dublin, where he complained that his Irish soldiers had run away. To which a lady replied, "I think your majesty has won the race."

While the Williamite war was waged up and down the country its issue was not one which touched the lives of the people in the way the previous Elizabethan and Cromwellian campaigns of extermination had done. To fight for the interests of an English king was an unfamiliar role for Irish soldiers, and in fact the most gallant deeds of this period occurred when Irishmen defended their own cities against siege and destruction, from no matter whom the threat might come. Most famous were the defenses of Limerick and of Derry—the former against William's forces, the latter against James's.

First came Derry, in 1689. As James approached and its elders hesitated, the young apprentices took matters into their own hands, swung to the gates of their city, and the siege began. It lasted six bitter weeks and is an epic of courage and endurance. It was broken dramatically at last as a relief ship with supplies of food smashed through the boom which barred the river. The 'Prentice Boys were vindicated and history honors them.

William's siege of Limerick met with an equally desperate defense. All its citizens, men and women alike, united in holding its walls, and kept at bay an army thirty thousand strong. It was only after a second siege which lasted a month that the defenders under Patrick Sarsfield came to terms.

It had been a gallant resistance, and Sarsfield won eternal glory by a daring raid on a Williamite arms train some miles from the city. Stealing out at night with a few picked companions he passed through the enemy lines. According to tradition the password for the night was "Sarsfield," and when a sentry tried to halt him Sarsfield galloped on, with the cry, "Sarsfield is the word and Sarsfield is the man!" The munitions were blown up and Sarsfield became one of the heroes of Irish history.

He negotiated honorable terms of surrender for the besieged city, and among the conditions of the Treaty of Limerick was a promise of freedom from persecution for Catholics. Peace was restored, and the Irish leaders were given their freedom. Sarsfield and his companions set sail for the continent to seek a new field for struggle. The Flight of the Wild Geese, the people left at home called this exodus, and they awaited its results with apprehension.

> Farewell, Patrick Sarsfield, wherever you may roam;
> You crossed the seas to France and left bitter hearts at
>   home.

Their forebodings proved correct. The Treaty of Limerick was soon contemptuously broken by the Williamite regime, and the persecution of Catholics, who formed four fifths of the population, became more vicious year by year. Conversion to Protestantism was not the aim, but rather the deprivation of all civil rights.

The Irish soldiers abroad kept their hearts full of hate for the betrayal of Limerick. Fifty years later they enjoyed some slight revenge. An Irish Brigade which formed part of the army of France, demolished an English force at Fontenoy. In the words of Davis's ballad—the French forces are in peril—Marshal Saxe unleashes the Irish troops:

> "Lord Clare," he says, "you have your wish—there are your
>   Saxon foes!"
> The Marshal almost smiles to see, so furiously he goes!
> How fierce the look these exiles wear, who're wont to be so
>   gay,
> The treasured wrongs of fifty years are in their hearts today.

Into battle they went to the cry:

> "Revenge! Remember Limerick! Dash down the Sas-
>   senach!"

And in memorable fashion they succeeded.

> And Fontenoy, famed Fontenoy, had been a Waterloo
> Were not those exiles ready then, fresh, vehement and true.

In the Protestant north of Ireland William of Orange became in course of time a heroic figure. In Belfast to this day big pictures of King Billy on his white horse are painted on the gable ends of houses and every summer on the twelfth of July great processions in Belfast and the surrounding country celebrate the Battle of the Boyne. Over their sober costume of navy blue suit and bowler hat the citizens wear an orange sash, and the air echoes to the roll of drums. These are no ordinary drums. They are called Lambegs and are as big as a man can carry. A really spirited drummer will bang away until the blood runs over his knuckles.

The principal procession is to a place called simply the Field, at Finaghy outside Belfast, and is a piece of colorful pageantry. Violent speeches are made and Orange songs are sung, and though of recent years some of the violence has gone out of the Orange processions, there is always the chance that on the Twelfth, feelings will be roused and blood spilled.

✤ 11 ✤

Swift and Tone

T HE BIGGEST THING to happen in Ireland during the early years of the eighteenth century was the arrival, in Dublin, as Dean of Saint Patrick's Cathedral, of Jonathan Swift, one of the great men of all time. With intellectual attainments and literary skill to equal his great contemporaries, Pope and Dryden, he combined a passionate love for mankind and for justice. Honored throughout the world for the brilliant satire of his *Gulliver's Travels*, he was also worshipped by his neighbors, the poor of Dublin. Although these could not have been expected to understand his literary achievements, they deeply appreciated his generous spirit and his courage in battling on their behalf. At his death thousands of humble folk wept in the streets. Even today it is impossible to read without emotion the noble epitaph which he wrote for his own tomb. Translated from the Latin it reads:

> He lies where savage indignation can rend his heart no more. Go, traveler, and imitate, if you can, one who did a man's part in the defense of liberty.

Swift abhorred English injustice in Ireland, and in his celebrated *Drapier Letters* he poured his scorn on tyranny.

46

... for in reason, all government without the consent of the governed is the very definition of slavery: but in fact, eleven men well armed will certainly subdue one single man in his shirt.

Despite England's strict control over the affairs of the country, the English colonists who had come to Ireland to make their fortunes were in some ways as greatly victimized as the native Irish. Any effort to develop trade or industry was repeatedly frustrated for the English feared it would rival similar enterprises in England. So it happened that even in the puppet Irish parliament, which during the thirty-three years of George II's reign had seen no new election, an eloquent minority, calling itself the Patriot Party, came forward with demands that it should be allowed to have some political rights.

The Patriot Party was making slight progress towards the achieve-ment of its cautious objectives when it was overtaken by the tidal wave of the tremendous democratic movement which now shook two continents. In 1775 the news of the American War of Independence inspired Irishmen with hope. Not only were they stirred by its ideals, but they had a warm feeling of sympathy for the country which had given a new home to so many Irish exiles. Indeed the exiles took a very prominent part in the struggle—of the signatories to the Declaration of Independence four were Irish by birth and four of Irish extraction.

Faced by a critical situation the British government asked the parliament in Dublin to agree to the despatch to America of 4,000 of the troops which garrisoned Ireland, offering to replace them by German soldiers. Flood, the leader of the Patriot Party, accepted this proposal, and by doing so lost his position of influence and popularity since the people in general were wholeheartedly in favor of American independence. It became clear that England's difficulty was Ireland's opportunity, and young Henry Grattan stepped into leadership in Flood's place. Under his guidance concessions were won, and England's economic strangle hold was slightly eased—a development which caused panic and strong opposition among English manufacturers. But foreign affairs dominated the scene, and England, terrified of a Franco-American alliance and possible invasion, even went so far as to concede in 1778, the right of the Irish to raise an armed volunteer force.

Units of this volunteer army were responsible for the expenses of their own drilling and uniforms, and elected their own officers from among their ranks, while the state provided them with arms. The English government hoped that this force, composed as it was mainly of well-to-do Protestants, would not only safeguard the approaches to Britain, but would also help to control the restless countryside. The rapidly growing industrial population in England had resulted in a demand for food that could not be met by the home suppliers, so Ireland's export restrictions had been relaxed. Irish farm land had become more valuable, common grounds were being enclosed and rents were rising. Dispossessed and threatened peasantry gathered into secret societies, calling themselves Whiteboys, Steelboys, Oakboys and similar names, under the mythical leadership of Captain Rock or Captain Moonlight, to fight as best they could the trend which was squeezing them from their homes and livelihood.

But the volunteers, who soon numbered 80,000, were less concerned with fighting the battle of the wealthy landed proprietors than with creating opportunities for themselves. As the danger of invasion receded they took up the cry of "Free Trade" and campaigned for an end to the tariffs which had crushed Irish industry.

Popular feeling ran high. The volunteers met, drilled and passed resolutions. On the crest of this wave the Irish parliament, led by Henry Grattan, in April 1782 claimed the right to legislate for Ireland. The British government, defeated in America, made a strategic retreat. The laws depriving the Irish assembly of power were repealed.

In doing this, England was not taking very much of a risk. No electoral reform was involved. The government in Ireland could be altered only at the desire of the Lord Lieutenant. Elections to parliament were held at eight-year intervals, more than two thirds of the members being elected by "pocket boroughs" in which sometimes less than a dozen votes were sufficient. This meant that the assembly was in effect controlled by a small number of influential landowners.

The volunteers pressed for parliamentary reform, but Grattan was not prepared to force the issue. He put his faith in the good intentions of the English government, but it had found that there was no need to yield further. The volunteers were disarmed, their political influence waned, and no reforms were made. The Irish administration was, however, able to relax trade restrictions. Cotton and other industries developed briskly—some, like Waterford glass, to become world famous for their fine craftsmanship. Landlords also benefited—England needed wheat and prices rose to record levels.

But an irremovable government and an almost unalterable parliament left many dissatisfied, and in 1791 a new and strongly democratic political party came into being. It was called the Society of United Irishmen, and it took up the more extreme demands of the Volunteers for religious freedom and political equality. The outstanding figure in this movement was Theobald Wolfe Tone, whose noble aspirations were combined with such gaiety, energy and good sense as to make him the most loved personality in Irish history.

The Society was founded in Belfast, and grew quickly, but the persecution of its leading members soon made secrecy necessary. Tone himself had to fly to America for safety in 1795, but within a few months he crossed the Atlantic once more and continued to work for his cause in France. The French government did in fact send a small force to the west coast of Ireland in 1796, but bad weather scattered the ships and no landing was made. The Irish revolutionaries confidently awaited a French invasion of England, which would be of great advantage to them, and during the winter of 1797

tremendous preparations were under way at home. All over the
country a citizen army was in training, and country blacksmiths were
busy forging crude weapons. Hopes were high—and then in 1798
Napoleon led his great forces not to Britain but to Egypt.

Some half million men had taken the oath of the United Irishmen, and no matter what might happen abroad this tide could be
held back no longer. Tension was rising, informers were at work,
and leaders were threatened with arrest. In May 1798 the insur-
rection broke out.

✤ 12 ✤

Seventeen Ninety-Eight

They rose in dark and evil days
To right their native land.
—JOHN KELLS INGRAM

THIS REBELLION, their first democratic uprising, captured the imagination of the Irish people. Its history could be written in popular ballads.

In county Wexford the fight was strongest, the citizen forces being led by a priest, Father Murphy.

> At Boolavogue, as the sun was setting
> O'er the bright May meadows of Shelmalier,
> A rebel hand set the heather blazing
> And brought the neighbors from far and near.
> Then Father Murphy, from old Kilcormack,
> Spurred up the rocks with a warning cry;
> "Arm! Arm!" he cried, "for I've come to lead you,
> For Ireland's freedom we fight or die."

Young John Kelly was another Wexford hero.

> "Tell me who is that giant with the gold curling hair—
> He who rides at the head of your band?
> Seven feet is his height, with some inches to spare,
> And he looks like a king in command!"

"Ah, my lads, that's the pride of the bold Shelmaliers,
    'Mong our greatest of heroes, a man!
Fling your beavers aloft and give three ringing cheers
    For John Kelly, the Boy from Killann!"

Enniscorthy's in flames, and old Wexford is won,
    And the Barrow tomorrow we cross!
On a hill o'er the town we have planted a gun
    That will batter the gateways of Ross! . . .

Meantime martial law had been proclaimed throughout the
country, and 130,000 English troops terrorized the population. The
odds were overpowering.

    . . . the gold sun of freedom grew darkened at Ross
        And it set by the Slaney's red waves.

The revolt was crushed and its leaders slain. The hand-forged
weapons were hidden in the thatch for another day.

In Dublin the heads of the United Irishmen had been arrested—
Wolfe Tone himself was expected with reinforcements from France,
but was captured on the north coast and died in a prison cell.

The north, like Wexford, had risen in memorable fashion, and
keeps alive to this day the memory of its heroes—young Betsy Grey
from County Down who rode to battle at her brother's side and was
butchered by the Yeomen, and Tone's friend Thomas Russell, who
was hanged at Downpatrick jail. "The Man from God-knows-where"
he is called in the northern dialect ballad. He had passed quietly
among the people, organizing the revolt, going safely even where he
was not known or expected:

        Into our townlan', on a night of snow,
        Rode a man from God-knows-where.
        None of us bade him stay or go,
        Nor deemed him friend, nor damned him foe,
        But we stabled his big roan mare. . . .

Gold jewelry (2,000-500 B. C.)

Irish glass (late 18th and early 19th centuries)

DEPARTMENT OF EXTERNAL AFFAIRS, DUBLIN

Typical Irish cottage, County Antrim

View of Killarney

DEPARTMENT OF EXTERNAL AFFAIRS, DUBLIN

Young Aran fisherman weaving a belt

PHOTO I. T. A.

Farmhouse and fields, County Mayo

River Liffey and O'Connell Bridge, Dublin

PHOTO I. T. A.

PHOTO I. T. A.

Rock climbing, County Kerry

Rock of Cashel

Sailors of the Irish Navy at Cobh

Confirmation Day, Connemara

The Pond, St. Stephen's Green, Dublin

Round Tower, Glendalough

DEPARTMENT OF EXTERNAL AFFAIRS, DUBLIN

Cave Hill, overlooking Belfast

Meeting the steamer, Aran Islands

Modern airport and Aer Lingus plane

Twelfth-century Clonfert Cathedral, Galway

Hurling match at Croke Park, Dublin

Cooperative creamery in Kerry

Blarney Castle

DEPARTMENT OF EXTERNAL AFFAIRS, DUBLIN

Fields in Donegal

Galway cattle fair

PHOTO I. T. A.

Modern housing near Dublin

Custom House, Dublin (18th-century architecture)

Clifden. Connemara

He stays the night with these sympathetic uninquisitive folk, who are waiting for the word to take their pikes from their hiding places. A couple of years pass:

> For a wheen o' days we sat waitin' the word
> To rise and go at it like men.
> But no French ships sailed into Cloughey Bay,
> And we heard the black news on a harvest day
> That the cause was lost again.

The crushing of the revolt left the Irish parliament open to attack. Union with England was proposed in 1799 and was rejected, but the English government was determined and set to work immediately to clear the way. Bribery on a grand scale was instituted. Peerages were created wholesale to overbalance the House of Lords, while the influential votes which controlled the pocket boroughs were bought at prices ranging up to £45,000. And so, with vague promises to allay the fears of merchants and of Irish Catholics in general, England forced the passage of the Act of Union, which became law on the first of January, 1800.

One courageous spirit yet remained to make a bid for success where the United Irishmen had failed. This was Robert Emmet, too young to have taken part, as had his brother, in the rising of '98. A brilliant student of Trinity College, he continued doggedly on the path laid down by his elders. In 1802 he visited Paris and interviewed Napoleon and Tallyrand. Relations between France and England were strained to breaking point, and Napoleon was quite ready to encourage further bloodshed in Ireland. He went so far as to suggest a suitable flag for the national movement—a tricolor with the words "Republique Irlandaise" across it.

Emmet returned to Ireland and laid his plans for another rising, but an accidental explosion betrayed his activities prematurely. On a summer evening in 1803, with one hundred followers, he called on Dublin and the country to rise. There was no disciplined force to follow his lead, although the Wicklow men did what they could, and Emmet, twenty-four years old, was arrested, tried and hanged in the streets of Dublin.

> Hung, drawn and quartered, sure that was my sentence,
> But soon I will show them no coward am I,
> My crime is the love of the land I was born in,
> A hero I lived and a hero I'll die.
>   Bold Robert Emmet, the darling of Erin,
>   Bold Robert Emmet will die with a smile,
>   Farewell companions, both loyal and daring,
>   I'll lay down my life for the Emerald Isle.

Few Irish homes during the nineteenth century did not have a picture of his trial scene on their walls, with the young man delivering his speech from the dock—a speech which ends with the words:

> "When my country takes her place among the nations of the earth, then, and not till then, let my epitaph be written."

✤ 13 ✤

After Napoleon

WITH THE RETURN of peace to Europe in 1815 and the dramatic fall in grain prices, landlords, hoping to cut their losses by restocking with cattle and sheep, hastened to clear their lands of tenants who could no longer pay rents based on high wartime values.

But the number of people went on increasing, even while they were being squeezed off the best land. In England and America the towns were quickly expanding as populations grew, but in Ireland where industrial development was so ruthlessly suppressed there was nowhere for people to move, apart from what had formerly been considered waste regions. Further and further up the mountainsides they retreated, clearing rocks and heather to make small holdings, or they moved into soggy ground on the fringes of boglands.

These developments did not take place without protest. The ballad maker summed up the feelings of the people:

> There may be seen fine meadows green
>   And bullocks sleek and grand,
> Just get your pole and take a stroll
>   And clear them off the land.
>
> This land so kind was ne'er designed
>   By Providence on high
> To keep John Bull with mutton full
>   While the natives starve and die.

All over the country angry groups resisted as best they could—burning, breaking fences, maiming livestock. The cattle were their enemies.

But the pressure continued to increase and the despairing peasantry began to leave the country—first as migrants for a few months of the year, to do harvesting work in England and Scotland, and then for good. America as well as England offered a way of escape, and as life at home became more hopeless the young and strong from each family would cross the Atlantic, to toil and save passage money so that relatives might follow.

At first the emigrants were driven by lack of opportunity in their homeland, but almost immediately after the collapse of agricultural prices—in 1817 and again in 1821—there were partial failures of the potato crop, on which most families had come to depend. Disease and death from hunger followed, and terror of starvation hastened the stream into exile.

Almost the only sign in Ireland of nineteenth-century industrialism at this time was the building of railways, and considerations of military strategy had something to do with this. Communications were important in garrisoning the country, and the Grand Canal from Dublin to the Shannon, which was started in 1756, and took almost fifty years to complete, proved useful for troop movements during the rising of 1798.

A colorful enterprise in a gloomy period was the public transport service of an Italian print seller named Bianconi, who had settled in Ireland. From a modest start with one horse in 1815 he developed a system which thirty years later covered three thousand miles of Irish roads. First using artillery horses, which were used to drawing heavy loads and which were sold off cheap when the Napoleonic wars ended, he later evolved a speedy type of horse-drawn bus which would carry twenty passengers.

The first Irish railway was opened in 1834, and throughout the forties and fifties the network spread through the country. Bianconi shrewdly adapted himself to the new development, bought railway shares, and linked his own services profitably with those of the trains.

The railway system was built piecemeal, local landowners supplying capital for a strip of line, becoming directors of it, and traveling thereon at favorable terms. At one time there were almost forty individual companies, with ten times as many directors, but under pressure of competition from modern road transport almost all have now been merged into a single national system.

Against the somber political background of the first decades of the nineteenth century a showy figure emerged. A big athletic man, sparkling with life, quick in repartee, with a magnificent voice and the useful training of a lawyer, Daniel O'Connell came forward from his Kerry home to give a lead to the Irish people.

In spite of promises, the Union had brought no relaxation of the disabilities which practically outlawed the Catholic Church and denied its members opportunities for advancement, and O'Connell, himself a Catholic and a member of a Gaelic family, first devoted his great powers to the removal of this injustice.

His call for Catholic emancipation awakened an enthusiastic response throughout the country. To raise funds for the movement a subscription of a penny a month was asked, and was collected at church doors, and the response was so great that soon a thousand pounds a week was available for organizing purposes. Although influential families still regarded parliamentary constituencies as their private property, O'Connell was determined to achieve his objective by constitutional means. His confidence was justified when in 1826 the electors of Waterford defied the Beresfords and faced wholesale evictions to return to parliament a liberal candidate who supported the emancipation movement. After this the campaign gathered momentum and in 1829, although as a Catholic legally debarred from taking his seat, O'Connell himself was elected by the voters of County Clare.

The British government accepted the situation. During the same year it allowed the passing of an act which admitted Catholics to parliament, to commissions in the army and to high legal posts but, on the other hand, it deprived most of the small farmers who had supported the emancipation movement so warmly of the right to vote. As a result, their dubious value to their landlord as electors having ended, evictions proceeded more rapidly than ever.

Except for the fact that they now had a few sympathetic representatives in parliament, in general the people found themselves worse off. But the emancipation campaign had taught them their strength, and taking the initiative into their own hands they began here and there to resist the collection of tithes. These were taxes collected from every household, irrespective of creed, towards the maintenance of the established church, a Protestant church, called the Church of Ireland, to which only a fraction of the population belonged. One of the first parishes to resist payment was in County Carlow, where there were fewer than seventy established church members as compared with over five thousand Catholics. In other parts of the country dissenting Protestants were similarly penalized. Resistance grew until the collection of tithes became virtually impossible, and before another decade had ended an act was passed which at least moderated this injustice.

O'Connell disapproved of the violent and bitter tithe war; he preferred to achieve his objectives by parliamentary skill, playing off the English parties against each other. His next target was repeal of the Act of Union, but he wanted Ireland merely to be allowed to manage her own domestic affairs, and did not seek national independence.

He soon found that this aim had by no means the sympathy in influential circles that the emancipation issue had enjoyed, and his parliamentary tactics met with no success. Realizing that any degree of Irish independence was an objective closer to the heart of the humblest Irish citizen than to the most liberal English politician, he decided to use again the tactics of his previous campaign and draw every Irishman into the struggle. At first he met with suspicion and doubt from the disenfranchised peasantry, but such a cause could not be ignored. By 1843 he was holding all over the country a series of monster meetings which were attended by hundreds of thousands of people. When he arrived for his meeting on Tara hill the crowd was so huge and closely packed that his carriage could not pass through it, and he had to cover the last two miles on foot. By sheer weight of public opinion he hoped to win repeal, but the British government looked on calmly. Towards the end of the year they banned what was to have been the final and greatest gathering, arrested O'Connell and gave him a term of imprisonment. The climax had passed and nothing had been achieved.

O'Connell's days of leadership were over. For twenty years the great agitator had held the political stage almost alone—now as his powers waned new voices were heard. Critical, constructive and enthusiastic, a group of young men had in 1842 launched a weekly newspaper significantly called *The Nation*.

The Nation

When boyhood's fire was in my blood
 I read of ancient freemen
For Greece and Rome who bravely stood,
 Three hundred men and three men.
And then I prayed I yet might see
 Our fetters rent in twain,
And Ireland, long a province, be
 A nation once again.
—Thomas Davis

THE SPARK which set this fire alight was the spirit
of Thomas Davis, a young student of Welsh origin at Trinity College. He gathered round him some of the most vivid minds of his time, among them the remarkable Francesca Elgee, mother of Oscar Wilde, and James Clarence Mangan, one of Ireland's most loved poets in his own land.

Oh, the Erne shall run red
 With redundance of blood;
The earth shall rock beneath our tread,
 And flames wrap hill and wood;
And gun-peal and slogan-cry
 Wake many a glen serene,
Ere you shall fade, ere you shall die,
 My Dark Rosaleen!

Davis, together with John Blake Dillon and Charles Gavan Duffy, in founding *The Nation* provided an outlet for the talents of the brilliant group. The articles, songs and ballads which were published week by week were read eagerly at crossroads throughout the country to the illiterate peasantry, who memorized the stirring verses and felt their spirits rise.

> Princely O'Neill to our aid is advancing,
>> With many a chieftain and warrior clan;
> A thousand proud steeds in his vanguard are prancing
>> 'Neath the borderers brave from the banks of the Bann.

Davis himself and many of the contributors were not great poets, but they wrote their ballads deliberately to capture and kindle the imagination of a people defeated and discouraged. They began also the task of gathering together the fragments of the national heritage —urging the preservation of historic buildings, of the dying Gaelic tongue, of the ancient traditions of learning, music and balladry, and of the memory of the brave and gallant efforts of bygone days. They advocated national self-reliance, and the development of the material resources of the country.

Some went further. Fintan Lalor preached the downfall of land lordism, and national independence. John Mitchel advocated physical force against England, and wrote on such subjects as guerilla tactics to counter troop movements on the newly constructed railways.

With such ideas in the air it was not long before a political grouping was established about *The Nation*. This was known as the Young Ireland movement, but its platform was a fatally divided one, more romantic than practical, and repeated blows soon rendered it ineffectual. Davis's early death was followed by disastrous years of famine.

The Famine, which began with the failure of the potato crop in the summer of 1846, was undoubtedly the greatest catastrophe to befall Ireland; and in history there have been few more terrible.

The population had soared to the perilous height of eight and a half millions. Every available inch of ground was planted season after season with potatoes, which grew luxuriantly without the help of fertilizers or the protection of chemicals. On them the people lived.

Then during the summer days of 1846, over the whole country, in district after district the fleshy stems of the plants gave way, the leaves sank back into the earth, and the air was filled with the stench of decay. Here is an eyewitness account from William Steuart Trench, who had given up his job as a land agent and launched on farming on his own.

> Each day, from the time I first heard of the disease, I went regularly to visit my splendid mountain crop, and each day saw it apparently further advanced in course of arriving at a healthy and abundant maturity.
>
> On August 6, 1846—I shall not readily forget the day— I rode up as usual to my mountain property, and my feelings may be imagined when before I saw the crop, I smelt the fearful stench, now so well known and recognised as the death-sign of each field of potatoes. I was dismayed indeed, but I rode on; and as I wound down the newly engineered road, running through the heart of the farm, and which forms the regular approach to the steward's houses, I could scarcely bear the fearful and strange smell, which came up so rank from the luxuriant crop then growing all around; no perceptible change, except the smell, had as yet come upon the apparent prosperity of the luxuriant stalks, but the experience of the past few days taught me that all was gone, and the crop was utterly worthless.

A million people died of starvation. A further million left the country in despair—mostly to go to the United States. The stream of emigration, once started, continued to flow, so that in the course of the past hundred years some six million Irish men and women have left their native shores, and the population at home has been reduced to half its peak.

As for the Young Ireland movement, the British government arrested and transported its leaders, and the revolutionary effort expired in an ineffectual skirmish in County Tipperary.

As had happened so often before many of the exiled leaders, deprived of an opportunity at home, rose to distinguished positions in other parts of the world. John Mitchel became a newspaper editor in the United States, and published his vigorous *Jail Journal,* a book which has become an Irish classic. Gavan Duffy became premier of Australia and accepted a knighthood from Queen Victoria, while D'Arcy Magee in Canada became a cabinet minister, but his career was ended by assassination.

The next political move came from the exiles in the United States. Out of touch with the realities of the situation at home, but conscious of the fatal weakness of the Young Ireland movement, they planned to organize an oath-bound Irish republican army, drilled and disciplined, dedicated to the liberation of the country. This organization was known as the Fenian Brotherhood. An attempted rising in 1867 was not successful, except in so far as it kept alive the spirit of revolt against tyranny.

> See who come over the red-blossomed heather,
>   Their green banners kissing the pure mountain air,
> Heads erect, eyes front, stepping proudly together;
>   Sure freedom sits throned on each proud spirit there.
> Down the hill twining,
> Their blessed steel shining,
>   Like rivers of beauty that flow from each glen;
> From mountain and valley,
> 'Tis Liberty's rally—
>   Out and make way for the Bold Fenian Men.

✤ 15 ✤

A Nation Once Again

FTER THE FAILURE of the Fenian movement Irish political leadership swung back into the hands of the parliamentarians once more. Some of the Irish representatives in the British House of Commons decided to look for the establishment of a national assembly which would at least have authority to deal with local matters. The new policy was known as Home Rule, and in the general election of 1874, sixty of the candidates who supported it were returned—no doubt benefiting from the introduction of secret balloting a couple of years previously.

This bloc became known as the Irish Party, in which Charles Stewart Parnell, a County Wicklow landowner, soon took the lead. He was a master of tactics and used his party, as O'Connell had earlier tried to do, to exert pressure on one or other of the two powerful English factions. But his chief aim was, by setting a high standard of statesmanship and responsibility, to win Ireland's right to legislate for herself.

While Parnell and the Irish Party maneuvered at Westminster every parish at home was in a ferment. A further depresssion had hit agricultural Ireland in the 'seventies. First prices had begun to fall, then the harvests of 1877 and 1878 failed. Dread of famine returned, and bankrupt tenants were evicted from their holdings, but this time the peasantry were not so helpless and in 1879 rallied to the Land League which had been formed to fight for their interests.

The League was founded by Michael Davitt, who had been born during the famine and whose family had been forced to emigrate when he was a young boy. He had lost an arm in a mill accident in Lancashire, but had continued to study hard and to take a keen interest in Irish politics. He joined the Fenian movement, for which he served a prison sentence for eight years, but like Fintan Lalor he was convinced that no progress could be made in Ireland without land reform.

Parnell gave the support of his party to this movement to keep the peasantry on the land, and the resulting political pressure, combined with the fact that Ireland was no longer the profitable investment that it had been for Britain, made the Westminster Parliament give way. During the next few years a series of Land Acts were passed which eased the position of the small tenant farmer, eventually allowing him, by a system of hire purchase, to become the owner of his holding.

Meantime the Irish Party pressed for the establishment of an independent legislature, and at last, towards the end of his career, the old English liberal leader, William Gladstone, went so far as to introduce a Home Rule bill. His government was defeated on the issue, and though he raised it again a few years later Parnell's influence had in the interval waned and the Irish Party was divided. In 1891 Parnell died, and two years later Gladstone's Home Rule bill was defeated for the second time.

In spite of political frustration every other aspect of life in Ireland was being transformed. The farmers were at last secure on their land—free to improve their home, to plant gardens and paint their houses, to fertilize their fields and repair their fences, all without fear of rising rents, of the bad year that might have meant eviction. Even the occupants of uneconomic holdings, mostly in the west, were being helped by a new official body called the Congested Districts Board which had been established in 1891. The Board encouraged cottage industries such as tweed making or beekeeping, built roads and harbors and helped fishermen to buy boats and nets. These western districts, which had suffered most from emigration, were now benefiting, too, from the growing prosperity of the United States. Then and for generations to come loyal children and children's children remembered the people at home so well that whole communities were supported by "emigrants' remittances."

The new farm owners soon began to find difficulty in selling their seventy-pound firkins of homemade butter on the English market in competition with the standardized produce of Denmark and Holland, and a voluntary movement for the establishment of co-operative creameries was quickly successful. Small-scale production was combined with efficient manufacture—each farmer could bring his churns of milk to the creamery where butter was made and marketed under hygienic conditions. Now all the country's supply of butter is produced by the co-operative creameries.

Another aspect of the work of the Irish Agricultural Organization Society was the distribution to farmers at the cheapest possible rates of fertilizers, seeds and equipment.

While life in country districts was improving, the organizations of the industrial workers were on the march against sweated conditions in factories, the overworking of young people and other evils of the towns. In 1894 the Irish Trade Union Congress held its first meeting. That year fifty-one unions represented 10,777 members—the following year there were ninety-three societies representing a membership of 17,476.

A wave of optimism swept across the country. Confidence in the future was accompanied by enthusiasm for the achievements of the past, on which were to be built a distinctively national way of life.

Generations of war, conquest and poverty had left Ireland with almost no cultural heritage. A few wealthy families adopted on a provincial scale the lead given by England, but there was hardly a trace left of any native tradition of architecture, of furniture or household fittings, of clothing or of cookery. Music was confined to folk songs and simple dance measures.

As for literature, while a few Anglo-Irish writers such as Swift and Goldsmith lent distinction to the world of English letters, most of the people were Gaelic speaking and in any case illiterate. In their songs and ballads the Gaelic poets preserved some craft and tradition long after the more tangible arts had been destroyed, but even their modest efforts could not survive, and the last of them may be said to have died with the famine.

Up to the beginning of the century there were very few schools of any sort in Ireland, and none at all for the poor. Such children, if they were to learn anything, had to attend hedge schools. This meant sitting around the teacher by the side of the road, most often without books, and perhaps in physical danger, for the penal laws against Catholics decreed that a hedge schoolmaster was liable to flogging, transportation or even hanging. Padraic Colum has written of the plight of a scholar of these times:

> My eyelids red and heavy are,
> With bending o'er the smould'ring peat;
> I know the *Aeneid* now by heart,
> My Virgil read in cold and heat,
> In loneliness and hunger smart.
>> And I know Homer, too, I ween,
>> As Munster poets know Ossian.
>
> And I must walk this road that winds
> 'Twixt bog and bog, while east there lies
> A city with its men and books,
> With treasures open to the wise,
> Heart-words from equals, comrade-looks;
>> Down here they have but tale and song;
>> They talk Repeal the whole night long.

Lonely and loyal, the poor scholar remains at his post, teaching

> . . . by the dim rush-light
> In smoky cabins night and week . . .

In time the British government came to realize that with a suitable curriculum education could have a propaganda value in Ireland, and in 1831 a system of free primary schools was made available throughout the country. These schools, combined with the effects of famine, emigration and the growth of the towns, helped to hasten the disappearance of the Gaelic language.

Just as all the old learning and traditions seemed to be dying away two energetic scholars appeared to give them at least a place in history. These were Eugene O'Curry and his younger brother-in-law John O'Donovan, born about the beginning of the nineteenth century. They translated the ancient manuscripts which lay in Dublin's learned institutions, recorded local history, folklore and place names, and wrote and lectured on life in ancient Ireland.

The pioneer work of these two men and their successors unfolded before the English-speaking world a rich panorama from the past. The centuries-old manuscripts contained not only records of ancient history and laws, but also lively accounts of Irish men and women of prehistoric times. These tales had passed from generation to generation by means of the bards, until they had been written down after the coming of Christianity.

The first translations of these stories revolutionized the ideas of many Irish people. They discovered that instead of always having been plunged in misery and defeat their country had enjoyed a vigorous and colorful early history, for centuries far in advance of England in its culture. To re-create this golden age became a national ambition in which nearly everyone joined in some fashion.

The Gaelic League was founded in 1893 with the object of reviving the Gaelic language, in which the manuscripts had been written and which was then still spoken in the remoter parts of the country. As well as holding language classes and publishing material in Irish the League organized a type of competitive gathering called a *feis* in every possible center. Contests were held in the singing of folk songs, in step dancing, fiddling and storytelling—the pastimes of rural Ireland. The Gaelic Athletic Association organized sporting events at which hurling and Gaelic football were played.

Attempts were even made to devise a suitable type of national costume, and advanced young women wore a sort of cloak embroidered with spiral patterns based on the Celtic designs used in old manuscripts, and fastened at the shoulder with an imitation ancient brooch. But the men were conservative and would not co-operate by wearing kilts, which were the recommended equivalent.

Those who doubted the wisdom of trying to revive the general use of the Gaelic language were nonetheless impressed with the color and vitality it possessed even in translation. Students of literature next discovered that simple folk throughout the country were speaking a form of English which was full of Gaelic idiom. So while he himself was applying his poetic art to episodes from the translated legends, William Butler Yeats advised John Synge to leave his studies in Paris and listen closely to what Irish country people were saying. This Synge did, in Wicklow and on the Aran Islands, and produced a series of plays written in a heightened version of their ordinary speech—an experiment which was received by Dublin audiences with mixed feelings. These and Yeats's own verse plays were performed by the Irish Literary Theatre, founded in 1899, which a few years later became the Abbey Theatre and won world fame.

Although in all this activity there were many crosscurrents a feeling of national individuality and independence was created which stirred almost everyone, and gave rise to a fresh political movement. This, founded in 1906, was called Sinn Fein, a Gaelic term which simply means Ourselves, and which indicates the new sense of self-reliance. The driving force behind this was Arthur Griffith. Once again the proposal for a national assembly with power to legislate for local affairs was put forward, and as a result of pressure the British government in 1912 introduced a new Home Rule bill.

There was still strong Unionist feeling both in England and Ireland against such a move. This had been growing in the north of

Ireland as it waned in the south, because the north had developed large-scale industries such as linen milling and shipbuilding which depended upon trade with the British Empire. With this background, the fact that the northern population was predominantly Protestant was used to divide it from the south. Feelings ran so high that a volunteer corps was founded in the north, and its leaders threatened to resist Home Rule by force if necessary.

They were answered by the formation of the Irish Volunteers in the south, soon 150,000 strong. When the situation was at boiling point, the first World War broke out and the Home Rule bill was shelved. The Irish parliamentary party gave its support to Britain in the war.

A group of Volunteer leaders, however, refused to be deflected even by the war from their objective, and went ahead with plans for armed revolt against Britain. Under the eyes of a heavily armed neighbor it was impossible to make any large scale preparations. When the appointed day came only a handful of men took part, mostly in Dublin.

The revolt began on Easter Monday, 1916.

> As down the glen, one Easter morn,
>   To a city fair rode I,
> There armed lines of marching men,
>   In silence passed me by;
> No pipes did hum nor battle drum
>   Did sound its dread tattoo,
> But the Angelus bell o'er the Liffey swell
>   Rang out in the Foggy Dew.
>
> Right proudly high over Dublin town,
>   They hung out the flag of war,
> 'Twas better to die 'neath an Irish sky
>   Than at Suvla or Sudelbar. . . .

Heavily outnumbered by British forces, the insurgents surrendered on the following Saturday.

Irish civilians on the whole, no less than the British military authorities, were taken by surprise by this rising. While their reaction was still undecided, the British proceeded to execute the fifteen leaders of the revolt, by ones and twos and threes, over a number of days. On May third the visionary Patrick Pearse, education reformer and author of plays, stories and verse, died with two companions. The following day his brother Willie was among the victims. There was another execution on the fifth, four on the eighth and one on the ninth. On the twelfth MacDermott, crippled with arthritis, was shot, together with the labor leader James Connolly, who because of his wounds had to be propped in a chair to die.

As the methodical extermination of these respected and well-liked figures proceeded, a wave of revulsion swept the country, and as wholesale arrests of sympathizers accompanied the executions the people accepted wholeheartedly the ideal of national independence. Sinn Fein burst into new life, and when in December 1918 a general election was held three quarters of the new members of parliament were representatives of Sinn Fein. This time they decided against the policy of acting as an Irish fraction at Westminster. They constituted themselves into a national parliament and claimed to be the lawful government of Ireland. The new regime in opposition to the British administration set up its own law courts and police force, together with state departments of foreign affairs, publicity and local government. For an exciting period the country had two sets of rulers, but it was the republicans who were accepted by the people.

To counter this situation British military and police made continual raids and arrests, and soon a state of war existed. The army of the Irish Republic was a guerrilla army—its members might work unnoticed in the fields by day and at night carry out ambushes or raids on barracks. The people were so united in this struggle that it was almost impossible for the British to find their opposing forces, who after an engagement could melt into the surrounding countryside and never be betrayed. All the efforts of British secret agents could not find the leaders, among whom the most daring was Michael Collins. Collins, who was a big, striking-looking man, would walk openly about the streets of Dublin, right under the eyes of British agents who were searching for him.

The capture and execution of republicans added fuel to the flames, and a victim such as the boy Kevin Barry became immediately a national hero.

> In Mountjoy Jail one Monday morning,
>   High upon the gallows tree,
> Kevin Barry gave his young life,
>   In the cause of liberty;
> Just a lad of eighteen summers,
>   Yet no one can deny,
> As he walked to death that morning,
>   Proud he held his head on high.

Guerrilla warfare continued for two years, until the British government proposed a treaty. This was to give Ireland dominion status, similar to Canada, but some of the northern counties were to remain directly under British administration.

Although the Irish parliament endorsed the treaty by a narrow majority many people were deeply disappointed by its terms. A section of the republican forces continued to resist the new Free State government. In this bitter civil war many of the heroes of the Anglo-Irish struggle were killed, among them Michael Collins who was shot in his native County Cork.

Despite the bitter opposition from all parties in the Free State to to the treaty clause which provided for the partition of the country it had to be accepted. The Unionists of the north wasted no time in consolidating their victory, and in establishing a local parliament at Belfast, which rules as a subsidiary of Westminster.

In 1925 the southern government took the first big step towards building up the economy of the new state. This was the great hydroelectric project known as the Shannon Scheme. But national development proceeded slowly, in face of many difficulties. Then in 1927 the uncompromising republican elements, led by Mr. De Valera, at last entered the Dail, as the new Parliament was called. In 1932 Mr. De Valera became premier, and under his guidance industrialization began to move at a faster pace.

It has been said that at the time the Free State was established the economic development of Ireland was seventy years behind that of the leading countries of the world. Now, at last, the race to catch up had begun.

✤ 16 ✤

Ireland Today

ABOUT three million people live in the Republic. All citizens who have reached the age of twenty-one are eligible to vote in parliamentary elections. They elect 147 representatives to the Dail, a Gaelic word meaning assembly, which sits at Leinster House in Dublin and legislates for the country. The elections are carried out on an elaborate proportional system which ensures that every important political grouping is fairly represented, one result of which is that it is very difficult for any single party to obtain an overwhelming majority.

The three principal parties are: Fianna Fail—led by Mr. De Valera—Fine Gael, and Labour, the last being very much the smallest. The first two groupings came into being after the state was founded, and are based on the division of opinion which then took place as to the terms on which a settlement could be made with Britain. The interests of Fine Gael in the past depended on close association with Britain, and the party was prepared to continue to allow Ireland to act as food producer for her neighbor, who in return would supply her with manufactured goods. This policy had, of course, the support of the stock breeders, and also established Anglo-Irish commercial concerns.

Mr. De Valera's government, on the other hand, broke the old ties with the aim of giving a share in the benefits of modern industrialization to all parts of the country, and of escaping the old de-

74

pendence on British manufactures. This policy proved its value during the second World War, when the country was able to maintain its independence and to live to a great extent on its own resources.

Now after thirty years of freedom and various government changes there is general agreement on economic policy. The more conservative party has changed its name from Cumann na n Gaedhil, under which it first held office, and accepts the idea of industrial development. Localization of industry has been carried almost as far as it can be, and now the principal problem for all parties is how to increase productivity and improve the quality of the goods produced, both on the land and in the factory.

Nearly half the Irish people still depend directly on farming for their living, and many factories are based on farm produce, so the fertility of the soil is very important. Efforts are being made to improve it by means of national schemes of drainage and fertilization, rural electrification and the greater use of machinery, but the number of men working on the land is falling by about 10,000 each year. Production is mostly concentrated on the raising of cattle for export, with milk and butter, pigs and bacon, poultry and eggs, sheep and wool, coming next in importance. Nearly all these are produced on farms of fifty acres or smaller, and marketing is very haphazard, which is bad for the farmer.

This would all add up to a bad prospect if we did not know that the people themselves are making an effort to remedy conditions that leave the rural parts backward as regards conveniences and interests. There is the co-operative movement which aims at taking the farmer out of his economic isolation, and by allying him with other farmers, helping him to get better equipment and better marketing. This movement has been in existence for some time and has raised standards of living in many parts of the countryside. And there is a more recent movement which aims at affecting the countryside on its cultural as well as its economic and technical side—"*Muintir na*

Tire," "People of the Country." This organization which has now hundreds of parish guilds and councils promotes craftsmanship, games, dances, musical and dramatic entertainments.

Modern enterprises, like the Electricity Supply Board, Sugar Company, Aer Lingus, the airline company, and Irish Shipping, were initiated by the government, and are all more or less under national control. The railways and road passenger services have also been amalgamated in a government company.

Irish doctors and nurses are known all over the world but it is only recently that keen interest has been taken in health services at home. One barrier to progress has been the lack of suitable hospitals. Many of the existing ones were built over a hundred years ago—Dublin's famous Rotunda maternity hospital is over two hundred years old. But now new ones are being built fast, and in many provincial towns the finest buildings are the new district hospitals.

All children must attend school from the age of six until they are fourteen, and a network of free "national" schools is provided for them. At these schools the learning of Irish is compulsory—sometimes all other subjects are taught through the medium of this language.

There is no free system of secondary or university education, and nearly all the secondary schools with the exception of those run by Protestant committees are under the control of religious orders. These schools get some assistance from the state, in return for which they are obliged to teach Irish to their pupils.

The encouragement of the Irish language has been a matter of policy since the state came into being. Besides being compulsory in schools all civil servants are expected to have at least a sketchy knowledge of it. Public notices are printed in both Irish and English and street names are posted in the two languages.

The public does not support these efforts with any great enthusiasm and a visitor is very unlikely to hear Irish spoken. In a few remote districts there are still native speakers, but even in these communities the language seems to be dying out.

Irish, or Gaelic, was once a vigorous language but for centuries the official work of the country was carried on in English. Gradually the development of printing, colonization, industrialization, emigration and other factors speeded its adoption by the people generally. Apart from some fine poems, the last important written works in the Gaelic language belong to the seventeenth century.

In Northern Ireland all the emphasis is on the association with Britain. England's royal family comes on state visits from time to time, and the official flag is the Union Jack. Even to expose the green, white and gold tricolor of the Republic is to invite a police incident. The radio station is a regional transmitter of the British Broadcasting Corporation. No official interest is taken in the Gaelic language, although it is occasionally taught in schools, and in nationalist districts it is studied with defiant enthusiasm. British currency and postage stamps are used, while in the Republic although the units are the same—pounds, shillings and pence—the designs are different. Instead of Britannia and the monarch's head on the coins there is the Irish harp with a series of animals on the reverse side—a woodcock on the farthing (a quarter of a penny), a hen with her chickens on the penny, a salmon on the two-shilling piece. British coinage circulates in the Republic but Irish currency is not acceptable outside the Twenty-six Counties.

There are fifty-two members in the parliament of Northern Ireland, elected not by proportional representation as in the Republic, but by a single nontransferable vote cast by all eligible citizens who have reached the age of twenty-one. This system ensures that a large majority in the northern House of Commons is Unionist, although about one third of the voters are nationalist in outlook. A small minority gives its support to labor.

This parliament, which has its headquarters at Stormont, near

Belfast, administers all local affairs, but certain powers such as income tax and the control of armed forces are reserved to the British government at Westminster. Northern Ireland pays a share, known as the Imperial Contribution, to the central government.

Because of these legislative links the north has benefited from Britain's social welfare program. Educational services, for instance, are much better than in the Republic. After a free primary education to the age of eleven, children are offered free secondary schooling up to the age of sixteen, with opportunities for technical training, for which no fees are charged. As for health services, a resident is entitled to almost all medical and dental care either for nothing or for a very small payment.

Some of the chief differences in character between life in the two parts of the country are due to distinctive religious traditions. In the north, Catholics form a minority of about one third of the total population of 1,300,000, but in the Republic they have a majority of over 90 per cent. In the Protestant north, Sunday is observed in puritan fashion, with no cinemas, theaters or games, and even the children's playgrounds in public parks are securely locked. Sunday in the south, on the other hand, is a day of relaxation, and while religious duties are scrupulously attended to, it is the favorite occasion for important football and hurling matches, dancing, excursions and other entertainments, particularly in country places. The Republic, however, practices a stricter censorship of books and films than does the northern administration.

Most southern Protestants belong to the Church of Ireland, the Irish branch of the Anglican or Episcopal Church, once the official church but disestablished in 1870, and this small minority retains an austere tradition. In the north the Protestant majority is divided almost equally into Presbyterian and Church of Ireland members, with a small number of Methodists and Unitarians.

Officially the governments of the Republic and Northern Ireland regard each other with grim disapproval, but the country is small for differences and, in fact, economic pressure is forcing co-operation. The Great Northern Railway, operating on both sides of the border, is a joint responsibility, while the Stormont government has helped to facilitate the building by the Republic of a hydroelectric power station on the river Erne, which drains a lake in northern territory.

None of the churches recognizes the division, and the Trade Union Congress represents organized workers in both parts of the country. Young Farmers' Clubs, although with separate headquarters, hold similar contests in plowing, cattle judging and other aspects of life on the land. The entries of the Armagh apple growers are conspicuous at the Autumn Fruit Show of the Royal Dublin Society. The rugby football team which represents Ireland in international matches is picked from the country as a whole.

As far as ordinary citizens are concerned the people of Belfast come in thousands to spend their holidays in Dublin, while southern tourists enjoy the splendor of the coasts and mountains of Antrim and Down. Young members of the international Youth Hostel Association cycling and hitchhiking during the summer find a chain of hostels open to them both north and south.

✤ 17 ✤

Dublin

In Dublin's fair city
Where the girls are so pretty.
—OLD SONG

THE OLDEST PART of Dublin is on a rise over-
looking the Liffey, in the neighborhood of the two cathedrals, Christchurch and St. Patrick's, which stand only a quarter of a mile apart.
The first was completed about 1038 by the Norse settlers who
founded the city a thousand years ago. Then when the invading
Normans arrived they lost no time in establishing a new cathedral
in order to counter the influence of the older church, and St. Patrick's was dedicated in 1191.

Although both cathedrals have been restored and added to during
the course of centuries, they remain the most ancient and historic of
Dublin's buildings. Lambert Simnel, pretender to the English
throne, was crowned in Christchurch in 1487, and for thirty years
during the first half of the eighteenth century Jonathan Swift was
dean of St. Patrick's.

When it was founded Dublin stood not only by the river Liffey
but also on the edge of marshy sloblands, and both the old Gaelic
names for the place are descriptive of the original site. The first was
Baile Atha Cliath, which means the hurdle ford, because at a shallow
place in the river there, chariots could be driven across if wicker

80

were embedded in the muddy bottom to make it firm. When the Norsemen came they were more concerned with a harbor than a ford and it became known as the Dubh Linn, or the black pool. By degrees as the city grew the swampland was reclaimed. In 1591 the university of Trinity College was founded on a site which had been the domain of sea birds, but is now the heart of the city.

Three hundred years ago there were barely ten thousand people in Dublin, but from that time it expanded steadily until in the eighteenth century it was listed as the seventh city of Christendom and enjoyed a period of glory until it was overtaken by the new cities of the industrial age.

The laying out of the present center of Dublin took place mainly about two hundred years ago. In 1757 a body called the Wide Streets Commissioners was set up, and the growing Irish capital was more carefully planned than almost any other town of its time. In the course of fifty years a series of magnificent buildings, public and private, was erected—the Four Courts and Customs House beside the river, the City Hall, the present frontage of Trinity College, the Parliament House in College Green which was acquired by the Bank of Ireland after the Union of 1800, and the Rotunda Hospital. The house built for the Earl of Charlemont is now the municipal art gallery, while the home of the Duke of Leinster has become the seat of parliament today. It was on Leinster House that James Hoban, an Irish architect who emigrated to the United States, based his design for the White House in Washington.

These white stone buildings in classical style are considered to be among the finest of their kind in the world. The ordinary dwelling houses of the period were built in brick, and followed a simple pattern. They relied for their effect on the vistas provided by the wide streets—sometimes straight with a view of the mountains at the end, sometimes curved, and varied here and there with tree-lined squares. The Wide Streets Commissioners were still in authority up to 1840, and building according to their regulations continued until then.

Most of these houses still stand, but some of the earliest near the center of the city have been demolished to make way for modern commercial buildings, while others have fallen into decay. The city corporation is anxious to preserve the character which was given to Dublin by the Georgian architects, and whole streets are now being reconditioned, keeping the external form of the original houses while making the interiors convenient according to modern standards.

A beginning is being made, too, in the erection of public buildings in a contemporary style. Best known is the airport terminal at Collinstown, but the newly completed bus station at Store Street is the most striking modern feature in the city itself.

Dublin is divided in half by the river, the most important link being O'Connell Bridge. Looking towards the sea from here you can see the funnels of the steamers in the port, but the Liffey dwindles rapidly so that the only traffic under the bridges is the fleet of small barges which plies between the docks and the brewery a couple of miles upstream. This brewery is one of the largest in the world and one of the city's principal industries. Although the quayside houses are crumbling with age they have been painted in all shades of fading colors and the view up the river sparkles.

Besides being geographically the center of the city, O'Connell Bridge is also a social center for Dubliners and visitors alike. During the day it is crowded with traffic, but in the evenings there are still hundreds of people crossing it and walking up and down O'Connell Street, the broad thoroughfare which rises from the river on the north side. Some of these are bound for theaters and movies, but there are many boys and girls in Dublin who come from the provinces and who live in lodgings with little to spend, who promenade here when their work is finished, hoping to see a familiar face from their home parish. The sidewalks provide modest entertainment for them—coffee or ices—to the sound of a juke box in the snack cafes, evening papers and pulp magazines spread for sale on the curb, while roving photographers snap the smiling, strolling passers-by. Commanding the street stands the General Post Office, which was for a week in 1916 the headquarters of the revolutionary forces. This remains open until a late hour, and crowds of dutiful or lonely youngsters use their pens and ink to scribble letters to their folk at home.

O'Connell Street is the scene of the biggest outdoor meetings during times of political excitement, but normally it sees its largest crowds on Sundays, when important matches are being played at the Gaelic Athletic Association stadium, Croke Park. Finals of Gaelic football or hurling championships bring special trainloads of supporters from the districts concerned, and for a few hours this part of the city is thronged, while tens of thousands of enthusiastic country people make their way to the sports ground and back again.

Many townspeople prefer association football, though this does not draw such immense crowds as the Gaelic games. Keen excitement is also aroused by rugby matches—this game is not widely played but every year Ireland is able to muster a team which can hold its own in the series of international games against England, Scotland, Wales and France.

Just off O'Connell Street stands the shell of the Abbey Theatre, which was recently destroyed by fire. Around this theater the Irish literary revival of fifty years ago was centered, and here were first produced the plays of Yeats, Synge and later, O'Casey. Many famous names were associated with the theater and its style of acting set a standard in its day. For years the Abbey has been officially subsidized, and a new building to replace the ruins of the original theater is being planned.

Across the river, in the library of Trinity College, lies the Book of Kells, the richly decorated eighth-century manuscript of the Gospels which has no equal in the world. Although its designs are mostly based on interlacing geometrical patterns, these are carried out in such varied forms and brilliant colors that they seem not formal but full of vitality. The work is so fine and delicate that nearly two hundred interlacements have been counted with the aid of a magnifying glass in one square inch alone.

Leading from Trinity to the public gardens and artificial lake of St. Stephen's Green is the narrow curve of Grafton Street, Dublin's most fashionable shopping district. Its restaurants and cafes are favorite meeting places for people with time to spare during the day. Nearby is the National Museum, where in the main hall are displayed treasures from the past and a variety of articles which indicate the manner of life of the early days—implements and ornaments from the stone age, such early Christian relics as the Ardagh chalice with its delicate silver tracery, replicas of elaborately carved Celtic crosses and church doorways, with explanatory charts and maps to fill in the background.

For human interest in the past the National Portrait Gallery has some curious and moving exhibits. Here are the death masks of Robert Emmet and Theobald Wolfe Tone—the long nose and face of the younger man contrasted with Tone's small features—and a charming wistful portrait of Swift's Stella, the young Esther Johnson. Beside her is Swift himself, but in a rather ponderous painting which does not bring to life his fiery spirit.

Perhaps life in the city can best be understood through the first-person account of a girl who lives there.

"My name is Maureen and I am seventeen years old. I work as a typist in a small office. This is my first job and I have had it for just over a year.

"Until I was sixteen I attended school at a convent near my home,—then I went to a commercial college to learn typing and book-keeping and shorthand. At first I studied these during the day, but when I began working I continued to go to evening classes. Now I have a certificate for one hundred and ten words a minute in short-hand and I would like to get as far as one hundred and twenty, but . . . Well, there are so many things to do in the evenings—tennis or cycling or a movie to go to, and I have just started dancing.

"Besides, I would like to study other things too—domestic economy, perhaps, or improve my French. I could go to classes in these during the winter at the local technical school. They would only take up three evenings a week.

"And I would like to join a musical society. I am very interested in music, especially singing. I listen to opera whenever I can—mostly on the radio, but two or three times a year there is a short season of opera in town. This year I saw *Madame Butterfly* and *Rigoletto.* There are always big crowds at the theater when opera is being performed, but if I queue long enough I can get into the gallery, high up where there are no proper seats, only steps to sit on. Here are often the keenest fans, and I'm told that long ago there used to be fine singers in the gallery audiences, who came regularly and entertained the house during the intervals.

"Altogether Dublin is supposed to have a great taste for singing —Handel's *Messiah* had its first performance here in 1742, in an old theater which stood in Fishamble Street, not far from where I work. A relative of mine was so enthusiastic that years ago he built in Dublin an opera house called La Scala, a smaller copy of the famous one in Milan. But he was disappointed,—it did not succeed. At the time many people only went to opera because it was fashionable and gave them an opportunity to show off fine clothes. Nobody wanted to buy tickets for the back seats. So Dublin's La Scala became a variety theater and then a cinema.

"Of course I like going to movies, too. In the evenings there is always a rush for the good ones, and if we don't want to queue for an hour my friends and I go straight from work at about six o'clock. This means missing a meal, but if we buy sweets and fruit and ices we can hold out until we get home. Anyway we always get a cup of tea in the office during the afternoon. In fact I hardly like to count how many times we drink tea during the day. First for breakfast. Usually a cup after lunch. Then twice in the office, at eleven and four. Next with the evening meal and perhaps again before bed.

"It is about two miles from my home to the office. When I started working I used to travel by the double-decker green city buses, but as I go home for lunch I found that the fares were taking up a lot of my wages. So I bought a bicycle. Dublin is full of cyclists, and there are a number of clubs. The boys and girls who are members go off in parties to the seaside or the country at week ends or on summer evenings. I might join one, but I see that most of the girls have very smart sports bicycles—blue and silver and all sorts of fancy colors. Mine is a homely looking one, painted black—not good enough for a club, I think.

"But anyhow it is useful just for traveling around the town. I can use it all the year, except for very few days when the rain is heavy or the roads are icy. And in the summer I can go with my friends to the sea—there are good sandy beaches only a few miles away.

"If I were to bring you to visit my home you would probably be surprised at the smallness of the buildings in the neighborhood. There are no blocks of apartments—every family has its own house and usually a bit of garden as well. But Dublin is spreading so fast now that people are beginning to worry about having to travel so far to work, and perhaps we shall have to get used to the idea of apartments before long.

"Our house was built about twenty years ago. It has a garden at the back with an apple tree and gooseberry bushes, and another little garden in front with a lawn which I sometimes have to mow.

"There are shops not far away, and my mother, like other Dublin housekeepers, just buys what she needs from day to day. Nobody has iceboxes, and though there are plenty of refrigerators on sale in hardware stores they are quite expensive and really not very badly needed in this climate. Our milkman leaves bottles of fresh milk every morning on the doorstep—it keeps all right until next day— and the shops get new supplies of fruit and vegetables, eggs and meat, two or three times a week.

"For cooking we use gas, and of course we have electricity as well. During the winter we burn coal or turf in open grates for heating, but fuel has been so scarce for a number of years that people have come to depend more and more on electricity to warm their houses.

"We have no telephone, nor have most of my friends unless their families happen to have a shop or business. But more people are installing them every day, and I suppose we will soon expect to have one in every house.

"Of course we have a radio, but there is no television service in this country yet. A few people have bought sets in hopes of seeing the English programs, but the distance is too great and reception is very bad. A TV network would be a big expense for a small country like this—in fact our only radio program isn't on all day. With sound broadcasting this doesn't matter because we can easily hear the British and West European stations any time we want them.

"During leisure time I go round mostly with my girl friends. Of course we are friendly with plenty of boys in the neighborhood or at work, but not specially so. A friend from Wales told me she was surprised at this—in her native city of Cardiff it is not uncommon for girls to marry before they are twenty. They just ask for permission to stay away from work for a day, get married, and are back on the job next morning. It's not like that in Dublin. Here an engagement is very cautiously entered into, a ring is presented and shown to friends and probably a party is given. The engagement lasts at least a year, while money is saved, a trousseau is collected, and a home found and furnished. A girl almost always gives up her job on marrying, which means that a young man must have a good and secure position before he can think of setting up a home on his own.

"To show you what a big effect this has on the lives of young people in Ireland, I believe the percentage of marriages among girls between the ages of fifteen and twenty-five is something like this: in Dublin 10%, Belfast 14%, while for England and Wales it is over 16%. As for the United States, I'm told that about forty per cent of girls are married by the time they are twenty-four. In country parts of Ireland even fewer girls get married than in Dublin.

"As far as clothes are concerned, my friends and I spend plenty of time discussing this subject but I must admit that we don't usually achieve very exciting results. By the time that we have got something that is tidy and practical for the office, suitable for the climate, and that won't be spoiled on the bicycle, we seem to be back again in the same old style pullover or blouse and cardigan and skirt. If someone were to count the cardigans in the country I am sure they would run into millions. The weather changes so suddenly here that even on warm summer days it is wise to carry a woolly which you can slip over your frock if the clouds roll up. We don't wear hats much except on Sundays, but often tie colored silk squares over our heads to keep our hair tidy.

"Well, if you want to know more about us, I hope you will come and see for yourself. You have probably often heard about Irish hospitality, and I think it really is true that we are friendly people. There has been a lot of talk about 'the tourist industry,' but the people who do come to spend their holidays here are always referred to as 'visitors,' as if they were friends of the family.

"So please come and visit us some time."

✤ 18 ✤

Round the South

Will you come to the land of O'Neil and O'Donnell,
Of Lord Lucan of old and the immortal O'Connell;
Where Brian drove the Danes and St. Patrick the vermin,
And whose valleys remain still most beautiful and charming.

You can see Dublin city and the fine groves of Blarney,
The Bann, Boyne, the Liffey and the Lakes of Killarney;
You may ride on the tide o'er the broad majestic Shannon,
You may sail round Lough Neagh and see storied Dungannon.

—OLD BALLAD

THE SMALL COUNTY of Wicklow which is south
of Dublin is called "the garden of Ireland" because of its lovely
scenery. There are mountains, lakes, rivers, waterfalls, cliffs and
sandy beaches— round every corner is a new and pleasant view. Even
the railway approaching it is delightful—it follows the sea so closely
that the trains seem almost to run along the strand.

St. Patrick landed at Wicklow itself when he came to Ireland as
a missionary in 432, but it was the Vikings who made a town of the
place and gave it a name. Vykinglo, they called it, the Viking beacon,
but gradually the name changed to its present form. Since those
days Wicklow has had plenty of associations with seafaring. In the
center of the town stands a monument to the memory of Captain
Robert Halpin, who in his ship the *Great Eastern* supervised the

laying in 1866 of the first telegraph cable to link Europe with the American continent.

Inland, a few miles away, lies the Vale of Avoca, which achieved fame during the last century through the popularity of Thomas Moore's song:

> There is not in the wide world a valley so sweet
> As the vale in whose bosom the bright waters meet.

In fact County Wicklow alone has several valleys with charms equal to those of the meeting place of the rivers, Avonmore and Avonbeg, but this district has a special interest because of its richness in minerals. It was here that prehistoric inhabitants found their supplies of gold—since then it has been worked for a variety of ores. The dumps from these workings, stained yellow with sulphur and ocre, purple, brown, blue and silver gray with other minerals, add to the picturesqueness of the scene. An old mill by the river houses a modern handweaving industry, and the designers of the brilliant woollen fabrics produced here, claim that their inspiration comes from the colors of the surrounding valley.

Here the mines are still being worked, but the neighboring valley of Glenmalure has only the ruins of mine buildings and workers' cottages. This desolate and impressive valley is almost uninhabited, and its steep rocky sides are normally deserted but for an occasional shepherd and his dog who pass along the skyline in search of their flock. But on summer week ends the cars and bicycles of city visitors crowd the rough narrow road to the head of the valley, fishermen stand along the banks of the shallow, rocky stream, and hikers prepare to walk over the mountain pass to the Glen of Imaal on the western side of the range or to climb the 3000-foot-high mountain, Lugnaquillia, highest peak of the Wicklow ranges.

In the unsettled past these mountains were the scene of bitter resistance to the invading British forces, and the lower end of the valley is dominated by the ruins of a massive stone barracks. Army engineers built a network of mountain roads, still called military roads, throughout the county to trap the rebellious Wicklowmen. Trees were cut then, too, to reduce the number of hiding places, but now the barren rocks of Glenmalure and many of the surrounding ranges are being planted by the Forestry Commission, and the quick growing pines are year by year altering the appearance of this countryside.

Even more popular with visitors is Glendalough, the next valley to the north. This is a deep cleft in the mountains, its sides so steep that except on the brightest day the waters of its two lakes seem dark and sinister. On a cliff overhanging the upper lake is an almost inaccessible ledge known as St. Kevin's Bed, where the sixth-century hermit is said to have lived for a time. Later he founded a religious settlement in the valley, the ruins of which, including a round tower, still remain.

Like other recluses of his time, Kevin was fond of the wild creatures, and, according to legend, when on one occasion in the course of prayer he happened to raise his hand towards heaven a blackbird alighted on it and laid her eggs on his outstretched palm. The saint remained patiently without moving his hand until the young were hatched.

South of Wicklow comes Wexford, the southeast corner of the country and most vulnerable to invading forces. The county town was another Norse settlement, and later the site of the first landing of the Norman warriors. From that time it remained close under the conquering eye of England. It absorbed the English language at an early stage, and based on this developed a distinctive dialect called Bargy which became almost a separate language and which has only died out within recent generations. But in spite of its early domination by the neighboring island Wexford retained a strongly independent spirit which showed itself in the rebellion of 1798, and also in its response to the rising of 1916.

Now one of the most progressive farming counties in the country, it produces one tenth of the national output of sugar beet.

Waterford is the most important harbor of the southeast—ford is a corruption of the Norse word fiord, an inlet—and its principal street lies along the quays. At one end of this stands Reginald's Tower, built in 1003. Here the Norman leader Strongbow, Earl of Pembroke, in 1170 married Eva, daughter of the king of Leinster—part of the payment promised for coming to her father's aid.

Waterford today is a brisk modern city, fourth in size in the Republic, with nearly 30,000 inhabitants. Among a variety of small industries such as meat canning, bacon curing and flour milling, which are supplied by the rich agricultural hinterland of Kilkenny and south Tipperary, an attempt is now being made to revive the glass industry for which Waterford was famed at the end of the eighteenth century.

Cork, next city round the coast, is the second in the state with a population of nearly 100,000. This is a gay and lively town, what it lacks in architectural distinction being amply made up for by the charm of its site. In it the River Lee branches so that at the end of every street there seems to be water, or if not water a hill—even a flight of steps. Much of Cork is built on a series of hills, and some of its suburbs look down not only on the central part of the city but also on the winding river channel, up which steamers make their way to dock almost beside the principal street.

Cork people are vivacious and sharp-witted, with quick singsong voices which please and amuse strangers. They take a passionate interest in the activities and enterprises of their southern capital.

Although national costume is almost unknown in Ireland, you may in the streets of Cork occasionally see a woman wearing a black-hooded cloak—a version of the mantilla and a relic of the Spanish tradition which was once strong in the small ports along this coast. The owner of such a hood would probably come from Kinsale, a colorful little fishing town with a tangle of narrow streets, and houses built in terraces stepped up a hillside, some still with an echo of Spanish style.

Five miles from Cork is Blarney Castle, a handsome fifteenth-century tower, once a powerful fortress but now famous of course for the Blarney Stone embedded in its walls. To kiss this means being held by the feet and leaning backwards over the parapet 120 feet above the ground. This is not so perilous as it sounds, for various aids have been built in, and a grating placed below in case of accidents. In fact the greatest hazard today is loss of dignity, but dignity is willingly sacrificed by enthusiastic seekers after the irresistible eloquence which the kissing of the stone is supposed to bestow.

The beauty of west Cork and Kerry is fabulous, but even the highest hopes are not likely to be disappointed. Nor can the wonderful vistas of lake and river, mountain and sea, ever become hackneyed by too frequent reproduction in photographs—the sparkle of the constantly changing atmosphere gives a special charm which must be seen to be appreciated. The rich and varied vegetation is an attraction in itself. A profusion of bamboos, palms, arbutus trees, scarlet fuchsia hedges, hazel, rhododendrons and mossy oak trees—these the remains of primal forests—grow to the brink of the lakes. Even bare rocks seem to nourish delicate plants, ferns and mosses—their existence being made possible by the mild moisture of the air. Sheltered by the trees and shrubs grow rare flowers, the mountain slopes above are carpeted with heather and yellow gorse, while even the bogs have a fascinating vegetation of their own.

Glengariff on the seacoast and Killarney inland are the best known centers. In spite of its location beside the Atlantic, Glengariff is a mild and sheltered spot, its bay dotted with rocky islets. At Killarney a series of lakes winds in and out at the feet of a rugged chain of mountains. The best views are from one of the roads which climb away from the town, or if you prefer you can hire a horse-drawn sidecar—an adaptation of Bianconi's "long car" on which travelers sit back to back—and drive by the lake shore. But remember Killarney's beauty owes a lot to its frequent rain and do not be surprised if you find yourself, together with driver, horse and car, sheltering beneath an arbutus tree while a shower passes.

Out on the promontories of this coast the salt Atlantic winds shear off the tops of stunted trees and bushes, and the atmosphere is fierce and exhilarating. Dingle Peninsula, as well as being the very end of Europe, is one of the most dramatic of these.

The town of Dingle itself is rather a sad little place now, with many of its houses empty and the harbor almost deserted. Long ago it was a busy port, trading wool and hides in exchange for Spanish cloth and wines, and in the eighteenth century it still had, like Kinsale, a Spanish air, with stone balconies to its houses. There are very few traces of that time left today. Set into the wall of one house is a stone inscribed with the date 1586—over another doorway are carved two stone birds, beak to beak.

Anyhow even by 1586 the Spaniards were having the worst of it. A little way ahead is the harbor of Smerwick, where in 1580 a garrison and settlement of six hundred Spaniards and Italians were massacred after their surrender to English forces, among whose commanders was that notorious Elizabethan courtier, poet and pirate, Sir Walter Raleigh.

The road to the west, around Slea Head, is carved out of the steep side of the mountain, and the Atlantic rollers boil on the rocks far below. The ocean stretches towards America until suddenly, round a last bend, three miles offshore, appear the Blasket Islands.

Of this scattered handful of rocks, only the Great Blasket is inhabited. Across the sound can be seen the tarred-roofed houses of the village, but they are emptying, for life here is too hard and perilous. Before this small community began to disintegrate, it had become famous as a still living example of an almost vanished way of life. It was visited by scholars and students who helped the people to record through their native Irish tongue a unique knowledge of primitive life and folklore.

At two o'clock in the afternoon of September 21, 1588, *Our Lady of the Rosary,* one of the crippled galleons of the Spanish Armada, drifted on the rocks between the islands and the mainland and sank with all her starving crew. Next day the *St. John of Ragusa* met with a similar fate, leaving one survivor, and two other ships narrowly escaped destruction. Watching from the cliffs were English soldiers, alert for any attempt at a landing, and the people of Dingle who must have seen with mixed feelings the fate of those with whom, but for the hazards of politics, they might have been trading peaceably as in years gone by.

All you are likely to see on these waters today are the canvas-covered canoes, called currachs, spinning lightly in the breeze as their owners fish for mackerel. Few travelers come here, but now and then a dusty touring car with English registration, noses its way slowly by; its passengers gaze at the view, and are pleased to hear occasionally the Gaelic greeting—"Dia's Muire dhiabh!"

This western tip of Europe is rich in remains of early Christian times—crosses, churches and the small stone beehive huts which were monastic cells. A signpost points to one of these, the primitive oratory of Gallurus. Away from the sea a rocky lane leads to an over-grown path, running with water like the bed of a stream and criss-crossed with brambles. At the end of this, across a stone wall, with the grass growing high around it, stands the little church, its thick dry stone masonry as perfect as when it was built, thirteen hundred years ago.

On the north side of the peninsula stands Brandon Mountain, one of the highest peaks in the country. This height is associated with the name of St. Brendan, born in 483, who according to legend was the first navigator to cross the Atlantic and the true discoverer of America.

Into Tralee Bay from the village of Castlegregory runs a sandy spit which has been found ideal for onion growing, and a profitable small industry has been established here. The handsome sand hills have become precious both for shelter and for cultivation, and to prevent the sand from drifting they are being painstakingly planted with closely placed clumps of coarse grass.

Now for a meal in the local hotel—fresh trout, soda bread and butter, and tea. But the little waitress is in a hurry.

"Where are you off to this evening—the movies?"

"Oh no!" with great disgust. "I can't *stand* them. There's a dance tonight. Till three."

"Oh. I suppose you don't have many late dances here."

"No indeed," she sighs. "Only twice a week. The other nights they finish at twelve." Her feet tap the floor impatiently as she clears away the dishes.

It is getting dusk. The roads are quiet. But what is this passing? It looks like a tractor—it *is* a tractor. Where is it going at this time of day? And why are there three young men—one on the seat, the others on a sack stuffed with hay—riding on it, dressed in their best?

You've guessed. This is Sunday evening in Kerry, and they're going to the dance.

✤ 19 ✤

By the Banks of the Shannon

The spacious Shannon spreading like a sea.
—Spenser

THE SHANNON, two hundred miles long, is Ireland's biggest river. Before trains and planes and motor buses it was a highway, and you might once have made part of your holiday journey on the *Mermaid* or the *Flying Huntsman,* or another of the paddle steamers which called at little harbors up and down the river. As long ago as May, 1829, the Dublin and Limerick Steam Navigation Company was announcing that it had provided

> a steam vessel of the first class for the lower Shannon, which will commence plying between Limerick and Kilrush on the 21st instant, stopping at Tarbert, for the convenience of passengers to Tralee and Killarney, taking up passengers at Glin, Foynes Island, Begh Castle and other places on the Shannon.

Kilrush was the terminus, the last stop before the Atlantic, a place which had seen much history passing by. Here in 1588 one of the battered ships of the Armada had moored and, desperate for water, offered equal quantities of wine in exchange. But English soldiers were on the watch, and the dying crew had to put to sea again, unsatisfied.

Seven centuries earlier invading Vikings had come this way, and had in course of time made peace with the abbot and monks on the holy island of Scattery near by. This association led to the abbey

97

being sacked by Brian Boru, who considered that the monks were being more helpful than they need be to the enemies of their country. But in spite of the turbulent past the ancient belfry tower—125 feet high and the finest of its kind remaining—still stands erect on its grassy island.

Every epoch has left its mark along the river. On the south shore the most striking landmark is the Norman fortress of Carrigafoyle, with a doorway opening on a tidal creek so that it could be approached by boat. Like so many ruined strongholds it is now a shelter for livestock—a convenience but sometimes an embarrassment to local farmers, as when a cow clambered up the winding stone staircase and was found grazing on the grass-grown roof of the main hall. She had to be carried down on a mattress by as many strong men as could fit in the narrow stairway.

In some parts of the country concrete has been laid on the roof-less upper floors of such old castles so that dances can be held there—couples sitting out in the embrasured windows from which molten lead was once poured on the heads of the attacking enemy.

A little further up the river is the scene of the Colleen Bawn story. Dion Boucicault's play of this name was a boxoffice success in the United States as well as in Ireland during the last century, and the story was also the theme of Benedict's successful opera, *The Lily of Killarney*. The original Colleen Bawn (which simply means Fair Maiden) was a sixteen-year-old girl who was abducted by a local squire and brought here to live by the Shannon. After a few weeks she disappeared, and eventually her body, bound with rope, was found among the seaweed on the Clare shore. The young man was arrested and charged with her murder, for which he was executed.

A reporter at the trial, Gerald Griffin, was so moved at the pathetic story that he re-created it in a successful novel called *The Collegians,* transposing the setting of the tragedy to Killarney to avoid giving offense. It was this book which inspired the other works.

At Tarbert where the river narrows, was once an important depot for the shipment of grain. In cut stone warehouses almost as powerfully built as the Norman castles, precious wheat was gathered during the Napoleonic wars for export to Britain. Now the stores have been demolished to make way for a housing scheme but an old doorway remains with the owner's name and fateful date cut into the stone: "J. N. Russell 1848"—a year of famine and revolt. No wonder that a few yards away stands a bridewell, the bars now almost rusted away from its prison cells.

At Loghill the river slices across the narrow seams at the margin of the Munster coal field. This is one of the few places where the coal was ever worked, and from the river a square-cut opening in the rock shows the entrance to an old tunnel. Through this the coal was once barrowed from under the hill and at high tide tipped straight into waiting boats.

Instead of paddle steamers today transatlantic planes follow the course of the river to the international airport near Limerick. If you come to Ireland you are quite likely to follow this route, and your first sight of Europe may be the coast of Clare. Indeed the coast of Clare is one of the sights of Europe—in particular the cliffs of Moher, rising seven hundred feet sheer from the sea. It is exciting and terrifying to look over a ledge of rock at the creamy breakers far below, while myriads of puffins and other sea birds float on the air currents which swirl around the cliff face. The upward draft is so strong that if you throw your hat over the edge it will float back to you again— if you are lucky!

Limerick, the third city of the Republic, draws its prosperity mostly from the rich pasture lands which surround it. Its food processing trade is long established—Limerick ham is another way of saying the best ham. Limerick lace, too, was a product famous all over the world, but with the decline of handicrafts and changing fashions it has now almost disappeared.

But like other old towns, Limerick keeps renewing itself. At the time of the Williamite wars, at the end of the seventeenth century, one of King James's generals refused to take charge of the garrison on the grounds that the city was indefensible. It could be taken with roasted apples, he said—then under Sarsfield's command it withstood two desperate sieges. The gallant Limerick of that day has vanished almost without trace—even the handsome eighteenth-century terraces which followed, are crumbling day by day. But encircling the old, a new city is growing—colonies of houses with gay-tiled roofs and little gardens, factories and grain silos and, most important of all, the hydroelectric power station a few miles up the river.

Above the dam and at the foot of Lough Derg, largest of the Shannon lakes, is the village of Killaloe. Here once stood Kincora, the palace of Brian Boru, utterly destroyed in the raids which took place after his death. James Clarence Mangan translated the lament of Brian's bard, MacLiag:

> Oh, where, Kincora, is Brian the Great?
>   And where is the beauty that once was thine?
> Oh, where are the princes and nobles that sate
>   At the feasts in thy halls and drank the red wine?
> Where, Oh, Kincora?

At the other end of the lake, twenty-five miles away, is Portumna —a village of a thousand citizens with a national reputation for tidiness. It has a tiny public garden, trim and neat, and in the shadow of the neighboring church you may see a woman with brush and bucket washing down a statue. On every sill there is a window box, with neat bushes in tubs beside every doorway. Even in the window of the butcher's shop, among the joints of beef and mutton, there are quite likely to be pots of red geraniums.

The bridge at Portumna joins the provinces of Leinster and Connacht, and has almost the air of a national frontier. To the west lies the territory which for centuries was the least subject of all the country to foreign rule—"not water enough to drown a man, wood enough to hang him, nor earth enough to bury him," complained a

Cromwellian general. Barren and mountainous, it remained the most Gaelic part of Ireland, and parts of its seaboard are among the few places where the Irish language is still spoken today.

Its capital city is Galway, long ago one of the chief ports of western Europe. According to local legend the ships of Christopher Columbus called here before setting out to cross the Atlantic, and the great explorer himself is said to have prayed in the local church of Saint Nicholas. Certainly a Galway man, Rice de Culvey, took part in the famous voyage.

Galway races in the summer are one of the country's most popular festivals. There's a ballad about them:

> It's there you'll see confectioners with sugarsticks and
>   dainties
> The lozenges and oranges, the lemonade and raisins.
> The gingerbread and spices to accommodate the ladies
> And a big crubeen for threepence to be picking while
>   you're able.

(Crubeens are pigs' feet.)

The western part of the county, a tangle of mountains, rivers, lakes, islands and sea inlets, is called Connemara. It is a paradise for city holidaymakers, but in this romantic setting lie many of the poorest homesteads in Ireland.

A similar countryside stretches north of Connemara into County Mayo, where beside the sea stands Croagh Patrick. From this peak Saint Patrick is said to have carried out his legendary banishment of snakes from Irish soil, and for fourteen hundred years it has been a place of pilgrimage. On the last Sunday of each July, fifty thousand people scramble up the rocky slopes of the 2,500-foot-high mountain, to hear on the summit a series of masses which begin at dawn.

Back on the Shannon, at the heart of the country, is the town of Athlone. Near by is the national radio transmitting station, so that Radio Eireann is often referred to simply as "Athlone." This is a placid countryside of small hills and high hedges—"the most pleasing horizon in nature," thought Oliver Goldsmith, who was born and brought up in this neighborhood. He left Ireland as a young man but in 1770, not long before his death, he published *The Deserted Village,* a long poem inspired by the oppressed land of his childhood:

> Ill fares the land, to hastening ills a prey,
> Where wealth accumulates and men decay.

Below the town of Athlone lies the ruined grandeur of Clonmacnoise, one of the great cultural centers of early Irish Christianity. On a grassy hill on the east bank of the river stands a group of ruined churches, tombs and round towers—all that remains of the monastic settlement founded by Saint Ciaran in 538. From here scholars and missionaries once went through Europe, winning honor and respect for themselves and for the place where they had been taught. Alcuin, adviser to Charlemagne, emperor of the French, wrote in 789 to the abbot of Clonmacnoise a humble letter enclosing alms from himself and his sovereign, and begging to be remembered in his prayers.

Close by winds the Shannon, brimming through swampy flat grasslands. In Viking days the Norsemen made use of it to advance from their base at Limerick, and Clonmacnoise like other rich monastic settlements suffered bitterly from their raids. When in 838 the Viking Turgesius took control of the area his wife established herself in Clonmacnoise, delivering pagan oracles from the altar of its principal church.

Rolleston has translated the lines of a Gaelic poet who looked on the scene long after the storm had passed:

> In a quiet watered land, a land of roses,
>   Stands St. Ciaran's city fair,
> And the warriors of Ireland in their famous generations
>   Slumber there.

Present-day schemes of electrification, peat development and drainage are liable at any moment to uncover dramatic evidence of life in ancient Ireland. One of the most important archeological finds of the century is the lake city which was revealed by the draining of Lough Gara on the borders of Sligo and Roscommon. Dwellings built on hundreds of separate mounds completely surrounded by water comprised this primitive Venice of the west, of which the gondolas were dugout canoes. The earliest of these lake homes belongs to the period of the stone age, and are between four and five thousand years old.

In the distance stand the mountains of Sligo, with their strange sawed-off outline and loose screes spilling down their slopes. On the summit of the solitary hill of Knocknarea is a cairn to mark the tomb of Queen Maeve, heroine of the epic tale of the Cattle Raid of Cooley. This cairn, some 40,000 tons of stone, is one of Ireland's many unexplored relics of the past.

All around is a countryside made famous by the Yeats family— William Butler Yeats the poet, and his father, Jack the painter. W. B. Yeats is buried by his native mountain, as he directed.

Among the small hills of Cavan is the source of the Shannon, which officially starts in a pool called the Shannon Pot. The boundary of the Republic is not far away and the neighboring village of Swanlinbar is a frontier post. Swanlinbar has a mineral spring, whose curative waters were once popular with local sufferers. Their complaints seem not to have been of the most serious kind. According to a sightseer of the time the taking of the waters was often followed by music and dancing, or at least a stroll in "the enclosure tastefully laid out in pleasant walks," in the company of the "best families of the district." As the village numbered less than a hundred houses accommodation was a problem, and visitors sometimes had to sleep in their coaches.

But today the well is grown over and the pump room with its pleasant gardens has completely vanished.

✦ 20 ✦

Up North

NORTH OF DUBLIN lies Tara, the site of Ireland's first capital. With the development of Irish civilization in pagan times this became the national center, but after the middle of the sixth century its importance dwindled.

The halls and palaces which stood on the low grassy hill have long since disappeared. These buildings, lavishly described in the old Celtic tales, were of wood, and nothing remains of them today but their outline in mounds and trenches, which archeologists have lately begun to excavate. The banqueting hall, built in the style of a Roman basilica by the third century monarch Cormac, in which to entertain visiting dignitaries, was seven hundred feet long and probably the largest building of its time in Britain or Ireland. It was divided into forty-two chambers, allocated to various social grades and trades, including bards, chess players, judges, physicians, charioteers, flute players, harpers and drummers, goldsmiths and engravers, with one for the king and queen.

Although the glories of Tara have vanished, standing on this hill it is not hard to understand why pagan Ireland came to honor this site. To the east, not far away, is the sea, but within a semicircle of fifty miles radius lies some of the most fertile land in the country, bordered by the Carlingford hills and Mourne mountains in the north, the Cavan hills, the Slieve Blooms in the midlands, and in the south the Wicklow ranges. Five ancient roads led across this plain

—from Galway, from two points on the Shannon, from near Dublin, and from Armagh, ancient capital of Ulster.

The plains of Meath and Louth had been favored from earliest times—near the Boyne River stand the royal tomb of Newgrange and two other tumulous mounds, erected perhaps a thousand years before Tara's pre-eminence. Then as Christianity spread through the country some of its first and greatest settlements were in this district—Kells where the famous manuscript was prepared, and Monasterboice, both founded in the sixth century, while Mellifont established in 1142, was the first Cistercian monastery in Ireland.

This countryside was also the scene of one of the great cycles of Celtic legend—the stories of the Fianna. Cormac, founder of Tara's greatness, inspired by Roman example formed Ireland's first disciplined armed corps, the Fianna. Its members had to conform to a high standard of physical fitness, chivalrous personal behavior and intelligence. They had to be familiar with the elaborate rules for the composition of Gaelic poetry. On entering the organization they had to take certain vows: never to marry for money, but to choose a wife for her virtues and good manners, and never to ill-treat women; never to judge anyone by his possessions; and never to be intimidated by overpowering odds.

They did not spend their time so much in fighting as in traveling round the country, hunting deer, camping by huge fires, and engaging in various kinds of contests—not least of them about women, in spite of the regulations. The king himself planned to marry an attractive young woman named Grainne but she, preferring a handsome member of the Fianna, drugged everyone else during a feast at Tara and asked this Diarmid to elope with her. To do so was treachery to his vows, but it was also against the rules to refuse any request to a woman. So they fled together and were pursued all over Ireland; many remote spots are still remembered as their resting places. In the end they were caught, as Diarmid had anticipated. He was killed and Grainne made the best of the situation by marrying the king after all.

Although after Cormac's death the Fianna disintegrated it remained a lively tradition throughout the country for centuries; more and more stories being added to the original ones.

An even older cycle of tales surrounds the Ulster settlement of Emania, two miles from the present town of Armagh, which flourished from the third century B.C. but which waned in importance as Tara grew. The warriors at the court of Conor Mac Nessa, about the time of Christ, were known as the Red Branch. They had their own headquarters, a palace built of wood fastened with copper rivets, and ornamented with bronze, silver and gold.

The Red Branch was not so much an organized body as a collection of fierce individualists, the greatest of whom was Cuchulain. Among their adventures the chief was their resistance to the cattle raid of Cooley—a bitterly fought issue, cattle being the most valued form of wealth according to the standards of the day. The trouble had arisen over a bull owned by a County Louth farmer at Cooley, which Maeve, queen of Connacht, wanted to add to her herd. She sent representatives to Cooley to purchase the bull, but the farmer disliked their attitude and refused to sell. On hearing this, Maeve angrily led her army across the country to take the animal by force. This brought the Connachtmen to the borders of Ulster, where Cuchulain held them, fighting warrior after warrior in single combat while the northern army was mobilized. At last Maeve's army, having seized the bull, was forced to retreat. But when, after all the bloodshed, the new bull was introduced into Maeve's herd, he instantly attacked its old leader. For a day and a night they fought, until the brown bull of Cooley was victorious and set out for home with the remnants of his enemy hanging on his horns. He reached Cooley again, but spent and exhausted, and the story ends with his death.

Long after the disappearance of the Red Branch, Armagh was still held in such respect that St. Patrick chose it as the headquarters of the Christian church in Ireland. It became a great teaching center—at the height of its activity it is said to have had seven thousand students. These, many of whom came from Britain, studied not only the Bible but also classical Latin works, music and astronomy. Its monastic schools were broken up many centuries ago, but Armagh is still the center of the Irish church, being the seat of both Catholic and Protestant primates.

The best apple-growing district in Ireland, Richill, lies near the town, while on the County Armagh fringe of Lough Neagh is the village of Maghery, with Coney Island just off shore. It was emigrants from this village who gave New York's Coney Island its name.

Armagh is part of the Six County territory, and crossing the border between the Republic and Northern Ireland requires a customs examination for a long list of contraband goods, since a different set of trade restrictions is imposed by each administration. This barrier makes life difficult for many of the citizens of the bordering counties, and the varying prices north and south of the line are an encouragement to smugglers.

Although the border seems an arbitrary line, following the county boundaries through hills and valleys, fields and village streets, still it has its roots in history. Faint traces can still be seen of an ancient defensive system, a thirty-foot-wide trench called the Black Pig's Dyke which during the Iron Age sealed off the northern quarter of the country in a line somewhat similar to the modern boundary.

Northern Ireland is the home of Irish linen—the finest linen in the world. Everywhere you can see fields of flax, the graceful plants in full bloom looking too beautiful to be useful. They grow to a height of about three feet, blossoming with flowers of a delicate blue. But harvesting is very hard work, for the plants must be pulled by hand so as not to break the precious fibers. The longer the fibers the finer the quality of the linen.

After pulling, the plants are soaked in pools of water until the fibers become loose. Then they are carefully dried again and put through a scutching mill to separate fibers and waste. It is at this stage that the fibers take on the pale silky look which has given rise to the expression "flaxen hair."

Eventually the flax reaches the mills of Belfast or of the provincial towns, to be made up into damask, handkerchiefs, towels and many other fine products. Many of the women of Northern Ireland work in the linen industry and are proud of their skill and traditions. In the mills it sometimes happens that a particular machine will pass in course of time from the care of mother to daughter. Even in this great industry a personal pride and interest is still taken.

The brick linen mills with their tall chimneys give even the small country towns of the north a character quite different to the market towns of the south. So is Belfast totally unlike Dublin.

Belfast is a city built for work, not pleasure. It grew quickly during the nineteenth century as its industry developed. Clay was grubbed from its hillsides and made on the spot into brick, while narrow cobbled streets of small houses sprang up in the shadow of the mill chimneys and within sound of the shipyard gantries on the Queen's Island. But in the beauty of its setting Belfast can equal Dublin. Close around it stands a ring of steep hills, looking down on the waters of Belfast Lough, which is not really a lake but an inlet of the sea. It was on Cave Hill, one of these heights, that four of the young leaders of the rebellion of 1798—Wolfe Tone, Samuel Neilson, Henry Joy McCracken and Thomas Russell ("the man from God knows where" of the ballad)—made a solemn vow to save their country and assert her independence.

Belfast differs from the cities of the south also in being mainly Protestant. But in the past this never saved its citizens from persecution, and during the American War of Independence sympathy with America's struggle was strong. Excitement rose to fever pitch when in 1778 Paul Jones sailed into Belfast Lough, defeated a British naval vessel and seemed on the point of driving the British out of the town. The moment passed, but parades and meetings to express revolutionary ideas were held with increasing intensity until the crushing of the 1798 rising.

During the latter part of the eighteenth century many thousands of Ulstermen fled in search of freedom to America. One of these was John Dunlap, printer of the Declaration of Independence. Gray's, the little printing shop in which he served his apprenticeship, still stands in Strabane.

Belfast got its charter as a town in 1613, but for a long time Carrickfergus, further down the Lough, was a more important harbor. One of the finest Norman castles in the country was built here about 1200 and is still in good order. It was at Carrickfergus also that King William landed on June 14th, 1690, first step on his march to victory at the Boyne a month later.

Not far away are the ruins of the church at Kilroot where Jonathan Swift began his clerical career. A Church of England clergyman in a Presbyterian neighborhood, his congregation was small. He is said to have spent one Sunday morning bringing wheelbarrowfuls of stones from the beach to his church, and in this way attracted an inquisitive crowd to the building. Then he locked the doors and preached to them.

Far around the coast of Antrim runs a magnificent road, built by famine relief labor. It lies at the feet of striking cliffs, partly white limestone, partly black basalt. A series of lovely glens cuts back into the Antrim uplands. Across the sea, only fifteen or twenty miles away, the farmhouses on the Mull of Kintyre in Scotland can be clearly seen.

Five miles off the coast at Ballycastle, lies the island of Rathlin. Robert Bruce, Scotland's national hero, took refuge here in 1306, and it is in one of the island's caves that the famous incident of the spider is supposed to have occurred. The exiled leader is said to have taken heart from watching the patient creature repair a damaged web. At any rate eight years later he defeated the English forces at Bannockburn and reigned king of a liberated Scotland.

Marconi, inventor of wireless telegraphy, whose mother was an Irishwoman, made some of his early experiments in radio communication between Ballycastle and Rathlin.

The Giant's Causeway on this coast is one of the natural wonders of the world. Stretching half a mile into the sea towards Scotland it has nothing to do with giants or causeways, but is the result of a volcanic eruption. It is made up of a series of pillar-like rocks, mostly six-sided and fifteen to twenty inches across. These fit together in a honeycomb pattern as regularly as if they had been sculptured. They vary in height, a couple of the taller groups being known as the Organ Pipes and the Chimney Tops. The latter was fired on by a ship of the Armada, which mistook it for the nearby cliff fortress of Dunluce.

Now we have come to the county of Derry. Its capital, the second city of the north, is Londonderry, so called since 1609, when it was burned by the English and handed over to the corporations of the City of London, who changed its name from Derry to Londonderry. It came first into existence as a settlement when Saint Columba founded a monastery there. The name which he gave the spot means an oak tree. A bard of the twelfth century wrote a poem on Columba's feeling for the place, putting the words into the mouth of the saint. Here is part of Kuno Meyer's translation:

> My Derry, my little oak grove,
> My dwelling and my little cell,
> O living God that art in Heaven above,
> Woe to him who violates it.

But Derry came to be a center of struggle, a fortified city whose walls are now the best preserved of any medieval town of England or Ireland. They were battered for four months during the siege of 1689, and Derry is better remembered for war than for peace. The northern Unionists have a challenging partisan song:

Long may the crimson banner wave,
A meteor streaming airy,
Portentous of the free and brave
Who man the walls of Derry:
And Derry's sons alike defy
Pope, traitor or pretender;
And peal to heaven their 'prentice cry,
Their patriot—"No surrender!"

Today Derry's walls have been made into a promenade for peaceful citizens.

You have had a few glimpses at the island of Ireland and now it is time to say good-bye. It was from Derry that Saint Columba left these shores in 563, and perhaps you can join in his parting with a heart as affectionate as his.

There is a grey eye
That will look back upon Erin:
It shall never see again
The men of Erin nor her women.

I stretch my glance across the brine
From the firm oaken planks:
Many are the tears of my bright soft grey eye
As I look back upon Erin.

INDEX

113